The Lighter Side of Cakes

CLASSIC ANGEL FOOD CAKE

• PAGE 20 •

ONE-BOWL
CHOCOLATE
CHIPOTLE CAKE

• PAGE 31 •

SWEDISH-SPICE CAKE WITH HONEY GLAZE

• PAGE 25 •

VANILLA-BUTTERMILK CAKE WITH STRAWBERRIES

• PAGE 32 •

PLUM CRUMBLE CAKE

• PAGE 26 •

TEXAS SHEET CAKE

• PAGE 36 •

GUINNESS
GINGERBREAD
• PAGE 37 •

BLUEBERRY
BUNDT CAKE
• PAGE 55 •

SOUR CREAM STREUSEL
COFFEE CAKE
• PAGE 59 •

MINI CHOCOLATE LAVA CAKES
• PAGE 40 •

CARROT CAKE BUNDT
• PAGE 66 •

TRIPLE-LEMON BUTTERMILK POUND CAKE
• PAGE 46 •

CHOCOLATE BIRTHDAY
CAKE WITH CHOCOLATE
CREAM CHEESE FROSTING
• PAGE 69 •

CINNAMON GRAHAM BUNDT CAKE
• PAGE 47 •

ANGELIC RASPBERRIES AND CREAM CAKE

• PAGE 70 •

MAYAN CHOCOLATE
CUPCAKES

• PAGE 94 •

APPLESAUCE CAKE WITH CARAMEL FROSTING

• PAGE 78 •

CARROT
CUPCAKES
WITH LEMON
BUTTERCREAM

• PAGE 98 •

RED VELVET CUPCAKES

• PAGE 99 •

LEMONADE
CUPCAKES

• PAGE 89 •

GREEN TEA (MATCHA) CUPCAKES

• PAGE 100 •

VANILLA-GLAZED
LAVENDER CUPCAKES
• PAGE 102 •

LEMON LOVER'S
CHEESECAKE
• PAGE 116 •

CHAI CUPCAKES WITH
WHITE CHOCOLATE
CARDAMOM
FROSTING
• PAGE 105 •

SO VERY CHOCOLATE
CHEESECAKE
• PAGE 117 •

CHOCOLATE CHIP—ORANGE
CHEESECAKE
• PAGE 123 •

NEW YORK CHEESECAKE
• PAGE 111 •

BLUEBERRY CHEESECAKE
• PAGE 113 •

GERMAN CHOCOLATE CHEESECAKE
• PAGE 136 •

ENLIGHTENED
Cakes

Also by Camilla V. Saulsbury

Cookie Dough Delights

Brownie Mix Bliss

Cake Mix Cookies

No-Bake Cookies

Puff Pastry Perfection

Panna Cotta

Enlightened Chocolate

ENLIGHTENED *Cakes*

*More Than 100 Decadently Light Layer Cakes, Bundt Cakes,
Cupcakes, Cheesecakes, and More, All with Less Fat & Fewer Calories*

CAMILLA V. SAULSBURY

CUMBERLAND HOUSE
NASHVILLE, TENNESSEE

ENLIGHTENED CAKES
PUBLISHED BY CUMBERLAND HOUSE PUBLISHING, INC.
431 Harding Industrial Drive
Nashville, TN 37211

Cover design: JulesRulesDesign
Text design: Lisa Taylor

Library of Congress Cataloging-in-Publication Data

Saulsbury, Camilla V.
  Enlightened cakes : more than 100 decadently light layer cakes, bundt cakes, cupcakes, cheesecakes, & more—all with less fat & fewer calories / by Camilla V. Saulsbury.
      p. cm.
  Includes index.
  ISBN-13: 978-1-58182-626-5 (hardcover)
  ISBN-10: 1-58182-626-5 (hardcover)
  1. Cake. 2. Low-fat diet—Recipes. 3. Low-calorie diet—Recipes. I. Title.

TX771.S253 2008
641.8'653—dc22

                                                                                    2008016480

Printed in Canada
1 2 3 4 5 6 7 — 12 11 10 09 08

To my parents, Dan & Charlotte

CONTENTS

Introduction 3

1: Old-Fashioned and Feel-Good *Favorites* 17

2: *Bundt* Bliss 43

3: Layer *Cakes* 67

4: Cup *cakes* 87

5: Cheese *cakes* 109

5: Frostings & Other *Extras* 139

Index 167

ENLIGHTENED
Cakes

INTRODUCTION

LIFE IS FILLED WITH COUNTLESS LITTLE PLEASURES—cake is one of the very best of them.

Why wait for a special occasion? Sure, a triple-tiered lemon curd cake may be ideal for a birthday fête or bridal shower, but an impromptu batch of Mexican chocolate cupcakes is perfect for Sunday supper, and a plum crumble cake is tops for teatime.

Now, armed with your copy of *Enlightened Cakes*, you can have your cake and eat it too, all with significantly less fat and fewer calories.

Developing lighter cakes for this collection—lower in fat and overall caloric content—took a considerable amount of testing and experimentation. While cutting back on butter and oil in cooking can be relatively simple, baking is a different story. With baking, each of a recipe's ingredients has a distinct, yet interdependent, role. Fat, in particular, lends cakes moisture, flavor, and structure and cannot be reduced without altering the other ingredients of a recipe, as well as the assembly technique.

But take heart: Lightening cakes is possible, and *Enlightened Cakes* is delicious proof. I set about baking using a variety of techniques and ingredient substitutions for cutting back on fat and calories in a wide range of cakes. My goal was simple: create great cakes, without compromising flavor or texture. The result is more than one hundred recipes for irresistible cakes for every occasion.

Each recipe is unique and downright delectable. I think you will find the results are every bit as irresistible as higher-fat favorites—perhaps even more so. Moreover, each is a reminder that a cake needn't be complicated to be excellent. Whether you are a new or seasoned baker, you will find recipe after recipe that delivers impressive results, time and again.

There's even more to recommend these cakes. In every chapter you'll find plenty of nostalgic flavors—think chocolate, caramel, vanilla, spice, luscious fruits and, yes, butter—they're all here, just with lighter fat and calorie profiles. Included, too, are innovative twists and captivating new tastes, such as fresh herbs, bold spices, floral accents, even some sassy takes on those old favorites—all to provide you with an ever-growing number of contemporary options for your cake-baking pleasure.

Finally, I offer detailed ingredient information for stocking a cake-ready pantry, a list of different types and shapes of cake pans, and tips for storing your cake creations to preserve their flavor. Using my handful of hints, your cake baking will be streamlined and stress free.

May this collection inspire you to head to the kitchen to let the baking begin. The recipes will take you through every season of the year from more delicate spring and summer fruit favorites to deep into fall and winter entertaining with spice-scented, pumpkin-plumped, and cranberry-jeweled creations. I'll be wondering which will become your favorites as I fork up a buttercream-frosted treat of my own.

TOP 10 TIPS FOR ENLIGHTENED CAKE BAKING

Whether you're making Swedish-Spice Cake with Honey Glaze, Citrus-Scented Olive Oil Cake, Triple-Layer Coconut Cake, or a batch of Favorite Fudge Cupcakes, it helps to remember that baking is both an art and a science. Success with any recipe depends on carefully following the instructions and using the right equipment.

So always begin by reading through the recipe, checking that you have all the necessary ingredients, and then gathering together all of the needed equipment and cake pans for the job.

And for even greater assurance of success, follow my top ten tips for enlightened cake-baking:

1. Stick with the fats specified in the recipe. It may be tempting to reduce the fat content of a recipe further by substituting fruit purées or low-fat margarine for some of the fat.

Resist the temptation. A recipe that's put on a crash diet will most likely flop. And while making a fat replacement may have worked in previous recipes, no simple substitution exists that applies to all recipes.

Fats coat the protein in flour, helping to tenderize the crumb. Any fat that's removed from a recipe needs to be replaced in whole or in part with other tenderizing ingredients such as sugar or buttermilk. While a few recipes in this collection use a small amount of fruit purées in the batter (such as applesauce), none use large quantities of fruit purée to replace fat. The reason is simple: because doing so results in cakes with inferior texture and taste.

2. Stick with real sugar, not substitutes. Replacing sugar with sugar substitutes that are meant for baking may sound like a good idea for further reducing the calories in a cake, but the chances for success aren't great. That's because sugar does more than sweeten the cake; it also plays a key role in the development of the structure and mass of the recipe (i.e., artificial sweetener has significantly less volume than sugar and does not provide enough substance to a cake).

Sugar also acts as a cake tenderizer and actually works in place of some of the fat in lighter recipes such as those in this collection.

Also, the flavor of sugar changes as it's heated—unlike artificial sweeteners, it caramelizes in baking, deepening the finished cake flavors.

3. Measure flour with special care. It's always important to measure carefully when baking, but it's crucial with lower-fat baked goods. Because the ratio of fat to flour is reduced, a fraction more flour than what is called for can lead to gummy, dense, even inedible results.

To ensure a more accurate measurement, lightly spoon flour into dry measuring cups. One cup should equal 4.5 ounces. For even greater precision, consider using a kitchen scale to measure. Above all, avoid using the measuring cup as a scoop to remove flour from a bag or canister—this will compact the flour and force more flour into the cup than required.

4. Use fresh, unsalted butter for best results. Salted butter tastes delicious on morning toast and muffins, but it can very easily throw off the results of cake recipe. Why? Because almost every recipe calls for salt, since it is a flavor enhancer. Using salted butter in addition to the salt called for in a recipe will lead to an overly salty cake. Also, unsalted butter has a fresher, more delicious flavor.

5. Use room temperature eggs. For best results, bring eggs to room temperature before adding them to cake batter. To warm eggs quickly, place them (still in their shells) in a bowl of warm tap water for 5 to 10 minutes.

6. Avoid overmixing. When combining the wet and dry ingredients, don't overmix—simply stir until the batter is just moist. Excessive mixing can cause early formation and escape of carbon dioxide gas. Carbon dioxide is necessary for leavening, forming tiny air pockets, in a baked cake. Also, overmixing can overdevelop the gluten in the flour. While some of this protein is necessary for the normal texture of a cake, too much gluten can produce rough, chewy, gummy textured cake.

7. Check the oven temperature. Use an oven thermometer to double-check for the correct calibration. Most ovens (even new and expensive ones) have fluctuating oven temperatures that can wreak havoc on tender cakes. Invest in an oven thermometer (they are inexpensive) to check the temperature after preheating the oven—and do it every time you bake—to ensure a proper temperature. If your oven temperature is far off kilter, you may want to consider having the oven professionally recalibrated.

8. Check for doneness at the minimum baking time given. If a cake is not finished cooking after the minimum time, then place it back in the oven for some additional baking time. Cakes are done when a toothpick inserted in the center comes out clean.

9. Bake in the center of the oven. Bake cakes with the oven rack placed in the center of the oven, unless the recipe states otherwise. Bake only on one rack.

10. Cool pans on wire racks. Cool all cakes completely on wire racks, unless specified otherwise in the recipe. Frost cakes when they are completely cooled or the frosting will melt or slide off the cake.

THE ENLIGHTENED CAKE PANTRY

Flours

All-Purpose Flour: Made from a blend of high-gluten hard wheat and low-gluten soft wheat, all-purpose flour is a fine-textured flour milled from the inner part of the wheat kernel; it contains neither the germ nor the bran. All-purpose flour comes either bleached or unbleached; they can be used interchangeably.

Whole Wheat Pastry Flour: A fine-textured, soft wheat flour that includes the wheat germ. It can be used interchangeably with all-purpose flour in most recipes. In most of the recipes in this book I've used it in combination with all-purpose flour, but feel free to increase the proportion of the whole wheat pastry flour to replace more or all of the all-purpose.

It is extremely important not to substitute regular whole wheat flour for whole wheat pastry flour; the results will be coarse, leaden, and possibly inedible.

You can find whole wheat pastry flour at well-stocked supermarkets as well as natural food stores. Store it in a ziplock plastic bag in the refrigerator to prevent rancidity.

Cake Flour: Finely ground, soft white flour. It is low in protein, which means it will develop less gluten during mixing and yield particularly tender baked goods. For a quick substitute, replace 2 tablespoons of flour with cornstarch for each cup of all-purpose flour.

Sweeteners

Granulated White Sugar: Granulated white sugar is the most common sweetener used throughout this collection. It is refined cane or beet sugar. If a recipe in the book calls for sugar without specifying which one, use granulated white sugar. Once opened, store granulated sugar in an airtight container in a cool, dry place.

Brown Sugar: Brown sugar is granulated sugar that has some molasses added to it. The molasses gives the brown sugar a soft texture. Light brown sugar has less molasses and a more delicate flavor than dark brown sugar. If a recipe in the book calls for brown sugar without specifying which one, use light brown sugar. Once opened, store brown sugar in an airtight container or ziplock plastic food bag to prevent clumping.

Powdered Sugar: Powdered sugar (also called confectioners' sugar) is granulated sugar that has been ground to a fine powder. Cornstarch is added to prevent the sugar from clumping. It is used in recipes where regular sugar would be too grainy.

Turbinado Sugar: Turbinado sugar is raw sugar that has been steam-cleaned. The coarse crystals are blond in color and have a delicate molasses flavor. Turbinado sugar is typically used for decoration and texture atop baked goods.

Honey: Honey is the nectar of plants that has been gathered and concentrated by honeybees. Any variety of honey may be used in the recipes throughout this collection. Unopened containers of honey may be stored at room temperature. After opening, store honey in the refrigerator to protect against mold. Honey will keep indefinitely when stored properly.

Maple Syrup: Maple syrup is a thick liquid sweetener made by boiling the sap from maple trees. Maple syrup has a strong, pure maple flavor. Maple-flavored pancake syrup is not recommended as a substitute for pure maple syrup as it is corn syrup with coloring and artificial maple flavoring added. Unopened containers of maple syrup may be stored at room temperature. After opening, store maple syrup in the refrigerator to protect against mold. Maple syrup will keep indefinitely when stored properly.

Molasses: Molasses is made from the juice of sugar cane or sugar beets that is boiled until a syrupy mixture remains. Light molasses is lighter in flavor and color and results from the first boiling of the syrup. Dark molasses, dark both in flavor and color, is not as sweet as light molasses. It comes from the second boiling of the syrup. Light and dark molasses may be used interchangeably in the recipes in this collection. Blackstrap molasses is thick, very dark, and has a bitter flavor; it is not recommended for the recipes in this collection. Unopened containers of molasses may be stored at room temperature. After opening, store molasses in the refrigerator to protect against mold. Molasses will keep indefinitely when stored properly.

Fats & Oils

Butter: When it comes to flavor, nothing compares to real butter. But because it is high in saturated fat, it is used in small quantities throughout this collection. All of the recipes were tested with unsalted butter unless otherwise stated.

Fresh butter should have a delicate cream flavor and pale yellow color. Butter quickly picks up off-flavors during storage and when exposed to oxygen; once the carton is opened, place it in a ziplock plastic food bag or airtight container. Store it away from foods with strong odors, especially onions or garlic.

To melt butter, cut the specified amount of butter into small pieces, place in a small saucepan, and allow it to melt over the lowest heat setting of the burner. Once the butter has melted, remove the pan from heat and cool. To speed the cooling, pour the melted butter into a small bowl or glass measuring cup.

To soften butter, let the needed amount stand 30–45 minutes at room temperature. Cutting the butter into small chunks will reduce the softening time to about 15 minutes. If time is really limited, try grating the cold butter on the large holes of a cheese grater. The small bits will be soft in just a few minutes. Avoid softening butter in a microwave. It will typically melt at least part of the butter, even if you are watching it closely.

Canola Oil: Canola oil is a neutral-flavored vegetable oil pressed from rapeseed and is extremely low in saturated fat and quite high in monounsaturated fat. It is used extensively throughout this collection.

Nonstick Cooking Spray: Nonstick cooking spray is canned oil that has been packed under pressure and is dispersed by a propellant. It is flavorless, coats pans evenly, and allows for easier removal of the cooled and chilled cakes throughout this collection.

Nonstick Baking Spray with Flour: Nonstick baking spray with flour is the same as nonstick cooking spray, only with the addition of flour. It eliminates the step of greasing and flouring cake pans, saving time as well as significant fat and calories. It is especially useful for Bundt-style baking pans. The two most common brands are Bakers Joy® and PAM® For Baking. If you have ever had half of a cake fall out of the pan, you will never want to be without this product—it is a minor miracle.

Dairy & Eggs

Milk: Both low-fat and nonfat milk are used throughout the collection in a wide range of recipes. Be sure to note when low-fat milk is used—the extra fat is need in that recipe, so nonfat milk should not be substituted. Similarly, do not substitute fresh low-fat or nonfat milk for canned evaporated fat-free milk; the latter has a richness similar to cream that fresh milk does not.

Eggs: All of the fat in an egg is contained in the yolk. To reduce the fat in many of the recipes, I cut back on the whole eggs and substitute egg whites.

Select clean, fresh eggs that have been handled properly and refrigerated. Do not use dirty, cracked, or leaking eggs that may have a bad odor or unnatural color when cracked open. They may have become contaminated with harmful bacteria such as salmonella.

Cold eggs are easiest to separate; eggs at room temperature beat to high volume for use in such recipes as meringues and angel food cake. Note that all of the recipes in this book were developed using large, room temperature eggs.

Refrigerated Egg Substitute: Egg substitute is made from real eggs, but only the whites, so it has a fraction of the fat and calories of whole eggs. Vitamins and other nutrients that would otherwise be lost when the yolk is removed are typically added. This product can be frozen if unopened. Once it has been opened, it must be used within a week.

Low-Fat Buttermilk: Commercially prepared buttermilk is made by culturing skim or low-fat milk with bacteria. It has a distinctive tang that, when added to baked goods such as cakes, yields a tender, moist result and a slightly buttery flavor.

Nonfat and Low-fat Yogurt: Yogurt is acidic, like buttermilk, and tenderizes baked goods. It also makes an excellent substitution for sour cream in a wide range of recipes.

Reduced-Fat & Fat-Free Cream Cheese: All of the recipes in this book use "brick"-style cream cheese; the fat-free and reduced-fat (also called Neufchâtel) are typically sold in 8-ounce rectangular packages.

To soften cream cheese, unwrap it and cut it into chunks with a sharp knife. Let it stand at room temperature 30 to 45 minutes until softened. For speedier softening, place the chunks of cream cheese on a microwavable plate or in a microwavable bowl and microwave on high for 15 seconds. If necessary, microwave 5 to 10 seconds longer.

Fat-Free Ricotta Cheese: Ricotta is a rich, fresh cheese with a texture that is slightly grainy, but still far smoother than cottage cheese. It's white, moist, and has a slightly sweet flavor. The fat-free variety is readily available and adds considerable richness to baked goods and cheesecakes.

Canned Evaporated Fat-Free Milk: Produced by evaporating nearly half the water from fresh fat-free milk, this thick and slightly sweet product is an excellent option for replacing heavy cream in a wide range of recipes from desserts to sauces. It is best used in recipes that are cooked or that have other strong flavors to conceal the slightly cooked flavor of the milk.

Canned Sweetened Condensed Fat-Free Milk: Sweetened condensed milk has been a baking staple for decades, but the fat-free variety is relatively new to the kitchen. This is one of those rare products that does not suffer much—if at all—from losing its fat. It is readily available in supermarkets (the fat-free version typically has a green label).

Reduced-Fat & Fat-Free Cottage Cheese: Makes a great addition to cheesecakes when puréed in a food processor and combined with other flavorful ingredients.

Chocolate & Cocoa

Unsweetened Baking Chocolate: Typically sold in packages of 1-ounce or 2-ounce blocks, unsweetened baking chocolate is dark chocolate without any sugar added. If chocolate develops a white or gray sheen, it is not spoiled; rather, it has "bloomed," meaning that it got warm enough for the cocoa butter's crystalline bonds to break and re-form in irregular pattern ("fat bloom"); or water has condensed on the chocolate's surface ("sugar bloom"). Bloom does not damage the chocolate for cooking purposes, but may make the chocolate grainy and less palatable for eating plain.

Miniature Semi-Sweet Chocolate Chips: Miniature chocolate chips are a good way to distribute a lot of chocolate flavor, even when only a small amount of chocolate is used.

Cocoa Powder: Select natural cocoa powder (as opposed to Dutch process) for the recipes that call for cocoa powder in this collection. It has a deep, true chocolate flavor. Although cocoa powder packaging should state whether it is natural or Dutch process, you can also determine cocoa powder type by sight: if it is dark to almost black, it is Dutch process; if it is natural, it is much lighter and more typically brownish-reddish in color.

Flavor Enhancers

Fat has great flavor, so when you cut it back, you need to add some flavor back. The following are some of my favorite big, bold flavor enhancers used throughout this collection.

Instant Espresso Powder: Stronger than regular coffee powder, a small amount of this potent powder dramatically enhances the flavor of chocolate and cocoa. It is now available in most supermarkets.

Spices: All of the recipes in this book use ground, as opposed to whole, spices. Freshness is everything with ground spices. The best way to determine if a ground spice is fresh is to open the container and smell it. If it still has a strong fragrance, it is still acceptable for use. If not, toss it and purchase a replacement.

Vanilla Extract: Vanilla extract adds a sweet, fragrant flavor to reduced-fat baked goods and is particularly good for enhancing the flavor of chocolate. It is produced by extracting the flavor of dried vanilla beans with an alcohol and water mixture. It is then aged for several months. The three most common types of beans used to make vanilla extract are Bourbon-Madagascar, Mexican, and Tahitian.

Store vanilla extract in a cool, dark place, with the cap tightly closed, to prevent it from evaporating and losing flavor. It will stay fresh for about two years unopened and for one year after being opened.

Imitation vanilla flavoring can be substituted for vanilla extract, but it may have a slight or prominent artificial taste depending on the brand. It is about half the cost of real vanilla extract; however it's worth the extra expense to splurge on the real thing.

Zest: The name for the colored outside layer of citrus peel. The oils in the zest are intense in flavor. Use a microplane grater or the small holes of a box grater to grate the zest. Avoid grating the white layer (pith) just below the zest; it is very bitter.

Liqueurs & Spirits: Alcohol adds significant flavor and dimension to reduced-fat recipes. You needn't buy an entire bottle for a recipe; look for the miniature-size bottles (like the kind on airplanes) at liquor stores; they typically contain 2 fluid ounces (¼ cup) and are a frugal option.

Rose water: A distillation of rose petals that has the intensely perfumed rose flavor and fragrance. It is a popular flavoring in Middle Eastern, Indian, and Chinese cuisines and adds an exotic flavor to cakes and other baked goods.

Orange flower water: A perfumed distillation of bitter-orange blossoms, orange flower water is used in much the same way as vanilla and other extracts. It has a delicate, floral taste and fragrance that works especially well with citrus and honey. It is available at liquor stores and in the liquor or specialty foods section of some supermarkets.

Dried lavender: A relative of mint, lavender has violet flowers and green or pale gray leaves, both of which can be used in cooking and baking. Lavender is a highly aromatic herb and its flowers are becoming very popular in cooking. The key to using it in baking is to use the right amount; too much is very bitter or perfume-like, but the right amount produces ethereal results. It is available from herb and spice purveyors as well as many health food stores.

Measuring Ingredients

Measuring Dry Ingredients: When measuring a dry ingredient such as cocoa powder, sugar, spices, or salt, spoon it into the appropriate-size dry measuring cup or measuring spoon, heaping it up over the top. Next, slide a straight-edged utensil, such as a knife, across the top to level off the extra. Be careful not to shake or tap the cup or spoon to settle the ingredient or you will have more than you need.

Measuring Liquid Ingredients: Use a clear plastic or glass measuring cup or container with lines up the sides to measure liquid ingredients. Set the container on a counter and pour the liquid to the appropriate mark. Lower your head to read the measurement at eye level.

Measuring Chocolate: Chocolate packaged specifically for baking is typically sold in 1-ounce or 2-ounce increments, making it easy to measure the amount of chocolate needed in a recipe by the ounce. Premium chocolate bars are also sold in ounce increments (e.g., 1.5-, 4- , 5-, or 6-ounce); cut or break off the amount needed and then proceed with the recipe directions for chopping, melting, etc. A small kitchen scale is also a useful investment for accurate measurement of chocolate by the ounce.

Measuring Syrups, Honey, and Molasses: Measure syrups, honey, and molasses as you would other liquid ingredients, but lightly spray the measuring cup or container with nonstick cooking spray before filling. The syrup, honey, or molasses will slide out of the cup without sticking, allowing both accurate measuring and easy clean-up.

Measuring Moist Ingredients: Some moist ingredients, such as brown sugar, coconut, and dried fruits, must be firmly packed into a measuring cup to be measured accurately. Use a dry measuring cup for these ingredients. Fill the measuring cup to slightly overflowing, then pack down the ingredient firmly with the back of a spoon. Add more of the ingredient and pack down again until the cup is full and even with the top of the measure.

Measuring Butter: Butter is typically packaged in stick form with markings on the wrapper indicating tablespoon and cup measurements. Use a sharp knife to cut off the amount needed for a recipe.

$\frac{1}{4}$ cup = $\frac{1}{2}$ stick = 4 tablespoons = 2 ounces
$\frac{1}{2}$ cup = 1 stick = $\frac{1}{4}$ pound = 4 ounces
1 cup = 2 sticks = $\frac{1}{2}$ pound = 8 ounces
2 cups = 4 sticks = 1 pound = 16 ounces

Measuring Cream Cheese: Like sticks of butter, bricks of cream cheese are typically packaged with markings on the wrapper indicating tablespoon and cup measurements. Use a sharp knife to cut off the amount needed for a recipe.

Measuring Spices, Salt, Baking Powder, & Baking Soda: Use the standard measuring spoon size specified in the recipe and be sure the spoon is dry when measuring. Fill a standard measuring spoon to the top and level with a spatula or knife. When a recipe calls for a dash of a spice or salt, use about $\frac{1}{16}$ of a teaspoon. A pinch is considered to be the amount of salt that can be held between the tips of the thumb and forefinger, and is also approximately $\frac{1}{16}$ of a teaspoon.

Measuring Nuts: Spoon nuts into a dry measuring cup to the top. Four ounces of nuts is the equivalent of 1 cup chopped nuts.

Measuring Extracts & Flavorings: Fill the standard measuring spoon size specified in the recipe to the top, being careful not to let any spill over. It's a good idea to avoid measuring extracts or flavorings over a mixing bowl because the spillover will go into the bowl and you will not know the amount of extract or flavoring you have added.

Bakeware

Always use the baking pan size specified in each recipe. The wrong size baking pan may cause your creation to overflow, burn around the edges and bottom, or sink in the middle.

To check the width of a pan, measure across the top from inside edge to inside edge.

Use shiny metal pans for baking cakes. They reflect heat, producing a tender, lighter-colored crust.

Dark, nonstick baking pans or glass baking dishes are less than ideal for baking cakes because they absorb more heat, which may darken the color of the finished cake. All is not lost, however, if that's what you happen to have: simply reduce the baking temperature by 25°F.

Baking Pan Equivalents

4 cups	9-inch pie plate
	8 x 1¼-inch layer cake pan
	7⅜ x 3⅝ x 2¼-inch loaf pan
6 cups	8 or 9 x 1½-inch layer cake pan
	10-inch pie plate
	8½ x 3⅜ x 2⅝-inch loaf pan
	7½ x 3-inch Bundt or tube pan
8 cups	8 x 8 x 2-inch square pan
	11 x 7 x 1½-inch baking pan
	9 x 5 x 3-inch loaf pan
9 cups	9 x 3½-inch fancy tube or Bundt pan

10 cups	9 x 9 x 2-inch square pan
	11¾ x 7½ x 1¾-inch baking pan
	5 x 10 x 1-inch jellyroll pan
12 cups	9 x 3½-inch angel cake pan
	10 x 3¾-inch Bundt
	9 x 3½-inch fancy tube pan
15 cups	13 x 9 x 2-inch metal baking pan
18 cups	4-inch angel cake pan

Cake Storage

The trick to a long-lasting cake is proper storage. Stored properly, most cakes will keep up to one week in the refrigerator or at room temperature, or for as long as six months in the freezer.

Room temperature and refrigerator storage: Store one-layer cakes in their baking pans, tightly covered. Store multilayer cakes in a cake-saver or under a large inverted bowl.

If the cake has a fluffy frosting, insert a teaspoon handle under the edge of the cover to prevent an airtight seal and moisture buildup.

Cakes with frostings containing yogurt, sour cream, whipped topping, or cream cheese should be stored, uncovered, in the refrigerator.

Cakes containing very moist ingredients—such as apples, bananas, carrots, pumpkin, or zucchini—should be stored in the refrigerator during humid weather or in humid climates. If stored at room temperature, these cakes tend to mold quickly.

Plastic and rubber containers for cake storage: Plastic and rubber cake storage containers are available in almost every size and are ideal for preserving the freshness of any cake, whether at room temperature or in the refrigerator. They are also a boon for transporting cakes, whether across town or on a long holiday trek. They really are worth the small investment.

Look for containers for Bundt cakes, layer cakes, even frosted layer cakes and cupcakes, from the following purveyors:

www.wilton.com
www.rubbermaid.com
www.pamperedchef.com
www.tupperware.com

Freezer storage: Unfrosted cakes can be frozen for up to six months if well wrapped in plastic and placed in plastic freezer bags. Thaw in their wrappers at room temperature.

Frosted cakes should be frozen unwrapped until the frosting hardens. Once the frosting has hardened, loosely wrap in plastic wrap, then place and seal in a large freezer bag for up to two months. To thaw, remove the wrapping and thaw at room temperature or in the refrigerator.

Cakes with fruit or custard fillings do not freeze well because they become soggy when defrosted. Instead, freeze cake layers individually, then fill once defrosted.

Snack cakes, bundt cakes, pound cakes, and unfrosted cupcakes freeze and defrost particularly well if wrapped in plastic and then placed in plastic freezer bags. Snack-type cakes can be baked in disposable aluminum pans, cooled, then tightly wrapped in their pans for freezing.

1. OLD-FASHIONED AND FEEL-GOOD

Favorites

WARM PEAR AND WALNUT CAKE, CLASSIC ANGEL FOOD CAKE, TANGERINE CHIFFON CAKE WITH FRESH BERRIES, MAPLE SUGAR CHIFFON CAKE, LINZER CAKE, PINEAPPLE AND DRIED CHERRY UPSIDE-DOWN CAKE, SWEDISH-SPICE CAKE, PLUM CRUMBLE CAKE, STRAWBERRY SHORTCAKES WITH FRESH MINT, CINNAMON STREUSEL SNACK CAKE, DARK CHOCOLATE SOUFFLÉ CAKES WITH VANILLA CRÈME ANGLAISE, LEMON PUDDING CAKES WITH RASPBERRIES, ONE-BOWL CHOCOLATE CHIPOTLE CAKE, VANILLA-BUTTERMILK CAKE WITH STRAWBERRIES, CHOCOLATE FUDGE BROWNIE CAKE, STICKY TOFFEE PUDDING CAKE, BLACK AND TAN MARBLE CAKE, TEXAS SHEET CAKE, GUINNESS GINGERBREAD, BITTERSWEET CHOCOLATE GANACHE CAKE, BANANA CAKE WITH BUTTERSCOTCH ICING, MINI CHOCOLATE LAVA CAKES . . .

Warm Pear and Walnut Cake

Pears and walnuts often grow side by side in California's—my home state—wine-country orchards. The two ingredients make ideal partners in this comforting, old-fashioned dessert.

	NONSTICK BAKING SPRAY WITH FLOUR	¼	TEASPOON SALT
3	TABLESPOONS UNSALTED BUTTER	2	MEDIUM FIRM-RIPE PEARS (ABOUT
1	TEASPOON VANILLA EXTRACT		½ POUND), CORED AND SLICED THIN (DO
2	OUNCES WALNUT HALVES (ABOUT ½ CUP)		NOT PEEL)
½	CUP FIRMLY PACKED LIGHT BROWN SUGAR	2	TEASPOONS TURBINADO (RAW) SUGAR
⅓	CUP WHOLE WHEAT PASTRY FLOUR (OR	1	TABLESPOON POWDERED SUGAR
	ALL-PURPOSE FLOUR)		OPTIONAL: SMALL SCOOPS OF LOW-FAT
3	LARGE EGG WHITES		VANILLA ICE CREAM

Preheat oven to 425°F. Spray a 9-inch round baking pan with nonstick baking spray with flour.

In a small saucepan melt the butter over moderate heat, then cool slightly. Stir in the vanilla and set aside.

In the bowl of a food processor process the walnuts, brown sugar, and flour until nuts are ground fine.

In a large bowl beat the egg whites and salt with an electric mixer at high speed until they hold stiff peaks. Gently fold in nut mixture. Fold in butter mixture (batter will deflate). Spread batter into prepared pan. Arrange pear slices evenly over batter and sprinkle with turbinado sugar.

Bake 22–25 minutes or until a wooden pick inserted in the center comes out clean. Transfer cake to a cooling rack and cool in the pan until warm. Sprinkle cake with powdered sugar. Cut into wedges and, if desired, serve with low-fat ice cream. **Makes 9 servings.**

NUTRITION PER SERVING (1 WEDGE):
CALORIES 174; FAT 8.3G (SAT 2.4G, MONO 2.2G, POLY 3.1G);
PROTEIN 2.5G; CHOLESTEROL 10.8 MG; CARBOHYDRATE 24.2G.

Classic Angel Food Cake

Angel food cake—which is surprisingly simple to assemble—owes its ethereal lightness and fine texture to whipped egg whites. The volume of the cake continues to expand in the oven as a result of steam, which evaporates from the liquid in the egg whites. Savor it on its own, or use it as the base for trifles, tiramisù, or with fresh berries and cream (as pictured in the photo section).

1 CUP CAKE FLOUR	2 TEASPOONS CREAM OF TARTAR
1½ CUPS SUGAR, DIVIDED USE	¾ TEASPOON SALT
2 CUPS LARGE EGG WHITES (ABOUT 15), ROOM TEMPERATURE	2 TEASPOONS VANILLA EXTRACT

Preheat oven to 350°F. Set aside a 10-inch tube pan with removable bottom (do not grease or spray).

In a medium bowl sift the flour with ½ cup of the sugar.

In a large bowl beat the egg whites, cream of tartar, and salt with an electric mixer at high speed until soft peaks form. Gradually add remaining 1 cup sugar, beating on high speed until very stiff peaks form. Beat in vanilla. Fold in the flour mixture in 3 additions. Transfer batter to tube pan.

Bake 45–50 minutes or until cake is brown and crusty on top and tester inserted near the center comes out clean. Turn pan upside down and fit center onto slender bottle neck. Cool cake completely. Run a knife around the pan sides to loosen cake. Turn cake out onto platter. Cut into wedges. **Makes 10 servings.**

Variations

Rosewater Angel Food Cake: Reduce vanilla to ½ teaspoon. Fold in 1½ teaspoons rosewater along with the vanilla.

Chocolate Angel Food Cake: Reduce flour by 2 tablespoons. Sift in ⅓ cup unsweetened cocoa powder (not Dutch process) along with the ½ cup sugar and flour.

Citrus Angel Food Cake: Eliminate the vanilla. Add 1 tablespoon finely grated citrus zest (e.g., lemon, lime, orange, tangerine) with the egg whites. Fold in 1 tablespoon fresh citrus juice when the vanilla would have been folded in.

NUTRITION PER SERVING (1 WEDGE):
CALORIES 184; FAT .09G (SAT .01G, MONO .01G, POLY .04G);
PROTEIN 5.7G; CHOLESTEROL 0MG; CARBOHYDRATE 39.9G.

Tangerine Chiffon Cake

WITH FRESH BERRIES

Food historians generally credit Harry Baker, a Los Angeles insurance salesman, for the "invention" of chiffon cake in the 1920s. Mr. Baker sold the recipe to General Mills in the 1940s. This riff on his original creation—a cake with the richness of a butter cake and the lightness of sponge cake—tastes like the height of summer in each bite.

1 CUP SIFTED CAKE FLOUR	1 TEASPOON VANILLA EXTRACT
½ CUP SUGAR	2 LARGE EGG YOLKS
1 TEASPOON BAKING POWDER	6 LARGE EGG WHITES
¼ TEASPOON SALT	¼ TEASPOON CREAM OF TARTAR
1 TABLESPOON FINELY GRATED TANGERINE ZEST	1 TABLESPOON POWDERED SUGAR
	1 CUP FRESH BLUEBERRIES
¼ CUP FRESH TANGERINE JUICE	1 CUP FRESH RASPBERRIES
1 TABLESPOON CANOLA OIL	

Preheat oven to 350°F. Set aside a 10-inch tube pan with removable bottom (do not grease or spray).

In a large bowl whisk the flour, sugar, baking powder, and salt. Add the tangerine zest, juice, canola oil, vanilla, and egg yolk to the bowl. Beat with an electric mixer at medium speed until smooth, stopping to scrape sides and bottom of bowl. Set aside and clean the beaters.

In a separate large bowl beat the egg whites and cream of tartar with an electric mixer on high speed until stiff peaks form. Gently stir one fourth of egg white mixture into the batter; fold in remaining egg whites. Pour mixture into tube pan.

Bake 23–26 minutes or until cake springs back when lightly touched. Transfer to a cooling rack and let cool 5 minutes in pan. Remove cake from pan and cool completely on rack. Dust with powdered sugar. Combine berries in a medium bowl. Serve cake with the mixed berries. **Makes 8 servings.**

NUTRITION PER SERVING (1 CAKE SLICE, ¼ CUP MIXED BERRIES):
CALORIES 167; FAT 3.2G (SAT .53G, MONO 1.5G, POLY .82G);
PROTEIN 4.6G; CHOLESTEROL 52.9 MG; CARBOHYDRATE 30.3G.

Maple Sugar Chiffon Cake

At once rich and light, this All-American cake is a big bite of nostalgia. Think pancakes and syrup, all dressed up. The sweet maple glaze and toasty pecans team up on top for a crunchy, tasty embellishment.

1 CUP SIFTED CAKE FLOUR	2 LARGE EGG YOLKS
½ CUP PACKED LIGHT BROWN SUGAR	6 LARGE EGG WHITES
1 TEASPOON BAKING POWDER	¼ TEASPOON CREAM OF TARTAR
½ TEASPOON GROUND CINNAMON	6 TABLESPOONS POWDERED SUGAR
¼ TEASPOON SALT	3 TABLESPOONS PURE MAPLE SYRUP
¼ CUP FAT-FREE MILK	⅔ CUP COARSELY CHOPPED PECANS, LIGHTLY
1 TABLESPOON CANOLA OIL	TOASTED
2½ TEASPOONS MAPLE EXTRACT	

Preheat oven to 350°F. Set aside a 10-inch tube pan with removable bottom (do not grease or spray).

In a large bowl whisk the flour, brown sugar, baking powder, cinnamon, and salt. Add the milk, canola oil, maple extract, and egg yolks to the bowl. Beat with an electric mixer at medium speed until smooth, stopping to scrape sides and bottom of bowl. Set aside and clean the beaters.

In a separate large bowl beat the egg whites and cream of tartar with an electric mixer on high speed until stiff peaks form. Gently stir one-fourth of egg white mixture into batter; fold in remaining egg whites. Pour mixture into tube pan.

Bake 23–26 minutes or until cake springs back when lightly touched. Transfer to a cooling rack and let cool 5 minutes in pan. Remove cake from pan and cool completely on rack.

In a small bowl whisk the powdered sugar and maple syrup until smooth. Drizzle over top of cake and sprinkle with pecans. **Makes 12 servings.**

NUTRITION PER SERVING (1 SLICE):
CALORIES 167; FAT 6.4G (SAT .73G, MONO 3.5G, POLY 1.8G);
PROTEIN 3.3G; CHOLESTEROL 35.4MG; CARBOHYDRATE 25.1G.

Linzer Cake

All of the flavors of a traditional Linzer torte — a nut, spice, and raspberry jam tart — are present in this delicious cake. To imitate the lattice crust of the classic dessert, lay thin strips of paper in a lattice pattern atop the cake before sifting with powdered sugar—beautiful!

	NONSTICK BAKING SPRAY WITH FLOUR	2	TABLESPOONS CANOLA OIL
½	CUP WHOLE-WHEAT PASTRY FLOUR (OR ALL-PURPOSE FLOUR)	¾	TEASPOON ALMOND EXTRACT
¼	CUP ALL-PURPOSE FLOUR	4	LARGE EGGS, SEPARATED
½	TEASPOON BAKING POWDER	¾	CUP SUGAR, DIVIDED USE
½	TEASPOON SALT	⅔	CUP SEEDLESS RASPBERRY JAM
⅔	CUP WHOLE ALMONDS	1	TABLESPOON POWDERED SUGAR
2	TABLESPOONS FAT-FREE MILK	½	PINT (ABOUT 1¼ CUPS) FRESH RASPBERRIES

Preheat oven to 325°F. Spray two 9-inch round cake pans with nonstick baking spray with flour.

In a small bowl whisk the flours, baking powder, and salt.

Place the almonds in the large bowl of a food processor and process until finely ground. Add the milk, canola oil, and almond extract, pulsing to combine.

In a large bowl beat the egg whites until soft peaks form. Gradually add ¼ cup sugar, 1 tablespoon at a time, beating at high speed until stiff peaks form. In a medium bowl beat the egg yolks and remaining ½ cup sugar with an electric mixer at medium speed (no need to clean beaters) until pale yellow and doubled in volume (3–5 minutes).

Gently stir the almond mixture into the yolk mixture. Gently stir in the flour mixture until just incorporated. Gently stir one-fourth of the egg white mixture into batter, then gently fold in the remaining egg white mixture. Divide the batter between the prepared pans, spreading it to the edges. Gently rap the pans against the counter once or twice to settle the batter.

Bake 18–20 minutes until the cakes are lightly browned and a toothpick inserted into the center comes out with only a few moist crumbs attached. Transfer cakes to cooling racks and cool in pan 10 minutes. Invert cakes from pans onto racks and cool completely.

Place one cake layer, top-side down, on a serving plate; spread with raspberry jam. Cover jam with the second cake layer, top-side down. Sift powdered sugar over the cake. Decorate with raspberries. **Makes 12 servings.**

NUTRITION PER SERVING (1 SLICE):
CALORIES 181; FAT 4.1G (SAT .70G, MONO 2.0G, POLY .98G);
PROTEIN 3.2G; CHOLESTEROL 70.6MG; CARBOHYDRATE 33.1G.

Upside-Down Cake

This easy upside-downer gets two extra boosts of flavor: a touch of ground ginger in the batter and tart dried cherries in place of the more typical maraschino variety. Using canned, sliced pineapple keeps the preparation simple.

1 20-OUNCE CAN PINEAPPLE SLICES IN JUICE, DRAINED	1 TEASPOON BAKING POWDER
⅓ CUP FAT-FREE CARAMEL ICE CREAM TOPPING	1 TEASPOON GROUND GINGER
¼ CUP DRIED TART CHERRIES	1 TEASPOON VANILLA EXTRACT
5 TABLESPOONS UNSALTED BUTTER, MELTED	¼ TEASPOON SALT
⅔ CUP SUGAR	¼ TEASPOON BAKING SODA
2 LARGE EGGS	¾ CUP WHOLE WHEAT PASTRY FLOUR (OR ALL-PURPOSE FLOUR)
½ CUP LOW-FAT BUTTERMILK	½ CUP ALL-PURPOSE FLOUR

Preheat oven to 350°F. Spray a 9x9-inch square baking pan with nonstick cooking spray.

Press 9 pineapple slices between paper towels until barely moist; set aside. Reserve the remaining pineapple for use in another recipe.

Drizzle caramel topping over bottom of the prepared pan. Arrange prepared pineapple slices in a single layer over caramel. Sprinkle cherries in hollows of the pineapple slices.

Whisk the melted butter and sugar in a large bowl. Whisk in the eggs until well blended. Whisk in the buttermilk, baking powder, ginger, vanilla, salt, and baking soda until well blended. Add the flours, stirring just until blended (do not overstir). Gently spoon the batter into the prepared pan, covering the pineapple, cherries, and caramel.

Bake 28–30 minutes or until a wooden pick inserted in the center comes out clean. Transfer cake to a cooling rack and cool in pan 2 minutes. Place a plate upside down on top of the cake and invert onto plate. Cool completely. Cut cake into squares. **Makes 9 servings.**

NUTRITION PER SERVING (1 SQUARE):
CALORIES 267; FAT 8.3G (SAT 3.9G, MONO 3.3G, POLY .49G);
PROTEIN 4.0G; CHOLESTEROL 66.0MG; CARBOHYDRATE 45.5G.

Swedish-Spice Cake

WITH HONEY GLAZE

Looking for something other than pies and tarts for the chilly months? This all-purpose spice cake is perfect. The honey glaze keeps the cake moist while accentuating the Swedish blend of spices: cinnamon, cardamom, and cloves. It's great to have on hand all through the holiday season.

NONSTICK BAKING SPRAY WITH FLOUR	2 LARGE EGGS
¼ CUP PACKED LIGHT BROWN SUGAR	⅔ CUP PLAIN FAT-FREE YOGURT
3 TABLESPOONS FINELY CHOPPED WALNUTS	2 TEASPOONS VANILLA EXTRACT
1 TEASPOON GROUND CINNAMON, DIVIDED USE	½ TEASPOON BAKING SODA
	¼ TEASPOON SALT
¾ TEASPOON GROUND CARDAMOM, DIVIDED USE	⅛ TEASPOON GROUND CLOVES
	1⅓ CUPS WHOLE WHEAT PASTRY FLOUR (OR
5 TABLESPOONS UNSALTED BUTTER	ALL-PURPOSE FLOUR)
¾ CUP PLUS 2 TABLESPOONS SUGAR	3 TABLESPOONS HONEY

Preheat oven to 350°F. Spray an 8-inch square baking pan with nonstick baking spray with flour.

In a small bowl combine the brown sugar, walnuts, ¼ teaspoon cinnamon, and ¼ teaspoon cardamom.

Place the butter in a large microwave-safe bowl. Cover and microwave at HIGH for 1 minute or until butter melts. Whisk in the sugar, then whisk in the eggs until blended. Whisk in the yogurt, vanilla, baking soda, salt, cloves, remaining ¾ teaspoon cinnamon and remaining ½ teaspoon cardamom. Gently stir in the flour, stirring just until blended (do not overstir).

Spread half the batter into the prepared pan, then sprinkle with the brown sugar mixture. Carefully spread remaining batter over brown sugar mixture.

Bake 22–25 minutes or until a wooden pick inserted in the center comes out clean. Transfer cake to a cooling rack and cool in pan 10 minutes. Place honey in a small microwave-safe bowl. Microwave at HIGH until liquefied. Brush or spoon over the warm cake. Cut into squares. **Makes 9 servings.**

NUTRITION PER SERVING (1 SQUARE):
CALORIES 290; FAT 9.7G (SAT 3.9G, MONO 3.5G, POLY 1.7G);
PROTEIN 4.8G; CHOLESTEROL 65.3MG; CARBOHYDRATE 47.3G.

Plum Crumble Cake

This delectable dessert is reminiscent of a cake my friend Louisa used to make and share with me. The recipe was passed down from her mother, who hailed from Bühl in the southwestern part of Germany. According to Louisa, the cake was traditionally made each year during festival time to celebrate the German plum harvest, which is celebrated every year with a festival in Bühl. The one-bowl batter is covered with wedges of fall plums; a sprinkling of walnut streusel bakes into a crunchy topping.

	NONSTICK BAKING SPRAY WITH FLOUR
1	CUP ALL-PURPOSE FLOUR
⅓	CUP SUGAR
⅛	TEASPOON SALT
¼	CUP (½ STICK) CHILLED UNSALTED BUTTER, CUT INTO SMALL PIECES
½	TEASPOON BAKING POWDER
¼	TEASPOON BAKING SODA
⅓	CUP FAT-FREE SOUR CREAM
2	TABLESPOONS 1% LOW-FAT MILK
1	TEASPOON VANILLA EXTRACT
½	TEASPOON ALMOND EXTRACT
1	LARGE EGG
4	OUNCES (½ OF AN 8-OUNCE PACKAGE) FAT-FREE CREAM CHEESE, ROOM TEMPERATURE
2	TABLESPOONS POWDERED SUGAR
1	LARGE EGG WHITE
¼	CUP PLUM JAM OR PRESERVES
6	MEDIUM PURPLE OR RED PLUMS, PITTED AND QUARTERED
2	TABLESPOONS CHOPPED WALNUTS

Preheat oven to 350°F. Spray an 8-inch square baking pan with nonstick baking spray with flour.

Combine the flour, sugar, and salt in a bowl. Cut in the butter with a pastry blender or fingertips until mixture resembles coarse meal. Reserve ½ cup flour mixture for topping.

Combine remaining flour mixture with the baking powder and baking soda. Add the sour cream, milk, vanilla and almond extracts, and egg. Beat at medium speed with an electric mixer until blended. Spoon batter into the prepared pan.

In a medium bowl beat the cream cheese, powdered sugar, and egg white with an electric mixer at medium speed until blended. Spread mixture evenly over batter, then dot with preserves. Top with quartered plums.

In a small bowl combine the reserved ½ cup flour mixture and walnuts. Sprinkle crumb mixture over plums.

Bake 27–30 minutes or until cake springs back when touched lightly in the center. Transfer cake to a cooling rack and cool completely. **Makes 8 servings.**

NUTRITION PER SERVING (1 PIECE):
CALORIES 282; FAT 8.4G (SAT 3.6G, MONO 3.0G, POLY 1.3G);
PROTEIN 15.6G; CHOLESTEROL 44.8MG; CARBOHYDRATE 35.8G.

Strawberry Shortcakes

WITH FRESH MINT

I love the addition of fresh mint to the traditional strawberry filling in these shortcakes, but you can certainly choose to leave it out if you prefer. Any leftover biscuits make delicious scones the next morning.

4 CUPS FRESH STRAWBERRIES, STEMMED AND SLICED	¼ TEASPOON SALT
8 TABLESPOONS SUGAR, DIVIDED USE	¼ CUP (½ STICK) CHILLED UNSALTED BUTTER, CUT INTO SMALL PIECES
1 CUP WHOLE WHEAT PASTRY FLOUR (OR ALL-PURPOSE FLOUR)	½ CUP LOW-FAT BUTTERMILK
1 CUP ALL-PURPOSE FLOUR	1 TEASPOON WATER
1 TABLESPOON GRATED LEMON ZEST	1 LARGE EGG WHITE, LIGHTLY BEATEN
2 TEASPOONS BAKING POWDER	3 TABLESPOONS CHOPPED FRESH MINT
½ TEASPOON BAKING SODA	1 CUP FROZEN FAT-FREE WHIPPED TOPPING, THAWED

Preheat oven to 400°F. Spray a large cookie sheet with nonstick cooking spray.

In a large bowl toss half of the strawberries with 3 tablespoons sugar and let stand 5 minutes. Gently press strawberries with potato masher to release their juices, being careful not to crush them to a pulp. Stir in the remaining strawberries. Let stand at room temperature, stirring occasionally, 45 minutes to 1 hour.

In a large bowl whisk the flours, lemon zest, baking powder, baking soda, salt, and 4 tablespoons sugar. Cut in chilled butter with a pastry blender or fingertips until the mixture resembles coarse meal. Add buttermilk, stirring just until moist.

Turn the dough out onto a lightly floured surface. Knead lightly 4 times. Pat dough to a ½-inch thickness, then cut with a 3-inch biscuit cutter to form 8 dough rounds. Place dough rounds 2 inches apart on the prepared cookie sheet. In a small cup whisk the water and egg white, then brush over dough rounds. Sprinkle evenly with the remaining 1 tablespoon sugar.

Bake 12–13 minutes or until golden. Remove from oven and transfer biscuits to a wire rack. Cool completely. Stir mint into strawberry mixture.

Using a serrated knife, cut each shortcake in half horizontally. Spoon ½ cup strawberry mixture over bottom half of each shortcake. Top each serving with 2 tablespoons whipped topping and the top half of the shortcake. **Makes 8 servings.**

NUTRITION PER SERVING (1 FILLED SHORTCAKE):
CALORIES 287; FAT 6.9G (SAT 3.3G, MONO 2.6G, POLY .47G);
PROTEIN 14.5G; CHOLESTEROL 17.4MG; CARBOHYDRATE 44.8G.

Cinnamon Streusel Snack Cake

For cozy comfort, this cinnamon-scented cake is hard to beat. Wonderfully homey, it's equally good with afternoon tea, after a meal, or for breakfast with a cup of dark roast coffee.

NONSTICK BAKING SPRAY WITH FLOUR

¾ CUP WHOLE WHEAT PASTRY FLOUR (OR ALL-PURPOSE FLOUR)

½ CUP ALL-PURPOSE FLOUR

⅔ CUP PACKED DARK BROWN SUGAR

⅛ TEASPOON SALT

1½ TEASPOONS GROUND CINNAMON, DIVIDED USE

¼ CUP (½ STICK) CHILLED UNSALTED BUTTER, CUT INTO SMALL PIECES

½ TEASPOON BAKING POWDER

½ TEASPOON BAKING SODA

½ CUP LOW-FAT BUTTERMILK

1 TEASPOON VANILLA EXTRACT

1 LARGE EGG

Preheat oven to 350°F. Spray an 8-inch square baking pan with nonstick baking spray with flour.

In a medium bowl whisk the flours, brown sugar, salt, and 1 teaspoon cinnamon. Cut in butter with a pastry blender or fingertips until the mixture resembles coarse meal. Reserve ½ cup flour mixture for topping.

Combine the remaining flour mixture with the baking powder and baking soda. Add the buttermilk, vanilla, and egg. Beat at medium speed with an electric mixer until blended. Spoon batter into prepared pan.

In a small bowl combine the reserved ½ cup flour mixture and remaining ½ teaspoon cinnamon. Sprinkle streusel mixture over batter.

Bake 27–30 minutes or until cake springs back when touched lightly in the center. Transfer cake to a cooling rack and cool completely. **Makes 9 servings.**

NUTRITION PER SERVING (1 SQUARE):
CALORIES 169; FAT 6.4G (SAT 3.1G, MONO 2.5G, POLY .35G);
PROTEIN 3.1G; CHOLESTEROL 38.9MG; CARBOHYDRATE 24.9G.

Dark Chocolate Soufflé Cakes

WITH VANILLA CRÈME ANGLAISE

Perhaps one of the most popular desserts of the decade, these puffs of pleasure are surprisingly straightforward to prepare. No need to be intimidated by the crème Anglaise, either—it's just an easy vanilla custard sauce that can even be made in advance.

8	TEASPOONS SUGAR	3	TABLESPOONS CORNSTARCH
⅔	CUP PACKED LIGHT BROWN SUGAR	⅛	TEASPOON SALT
½	CUP WATER	2	LARGE EGG YOLKS
2	1-OUNCE SQUARES SEMISWEET CHOCO-LATE, CHOPPED	1	TEASPOON VANILLA EXTRACT
1	1-OUNCE SQUARE UNSWEETENED CHOCO-LATE, CHOPPED	4	LARGE EGG WHITES
		¼	TEASPOON CREAM OF TARTAR
½	CUP UNSWEETENED COCOA POWDER (NOT DUTCH PROCESS)	3	TABLESPOONS POWDERED SUGAR
		1	RECIPE VANILLA CRÈME ANGLAISE (SEE PAGE 164)

Preheat oven to 350°F. Lightly coat eight 4-ounce ramekins with nonstick cooking spray. Sprinkle each ramekin with 1 teaspoon sugar. Place ramekins in a large baking dish.

In a medium, heavy saucepan combine the brown sugar and water. Bring to a boil over medium heat, stirring to dissolve sugar. Remove from heat. Add chocolates, stirring with a whisk until chocolates are melted. In a small bowl whisk the cocoa powder, cornstarch, and salt. Whisk cocoa mixture, egg yolks, and vanilla into chocolate mixture until blended and smooth.

In a large bowl beat the egg whites and cream of tartar with an electric mixer at medium speed until soft peaks form. Gradually add the powdered sugar, 1 tablespoon at a time, beating at high speed until stiff peaks form. Gently stir one-fourth of egg white mixture into chocolate mixture, then gently fold in remaining egg white mixture.

Spoon batter into prepared ramekins. Add hot water to baking dish to a depth of ¾ inch.

Bake 15–17 minutes or until the cakes are puffy and slightly cracked. Remove the ramekins from the baking dish and place on a wire rack. Cool 10 minutes. Serve warm with Vanilla Crème Anglaise. **Makes 8 servings.**

NUTRITION PER SERVING (1 SOUFFLÉ CAKE AND ABOUT 1 TABLESPOON SAUCE):
CALORIES 278; FAT 7.5G (SAT 3.8G, MONO 2.5G, POLY .49G); PROTEIN 16.1G;
CHOLESTEROL 107.3MG; CARBOHYDRATE 41.1G.

Lemon Pudding Cakes

WITH RASPBERRIES

These elegant cakes have a soft pudding-like center and vibrant lemon flavor. Although scrumptious served warm, they can also be made ahead, refrigerated, then served at room temperature.

¾ CUP SUGAR	5 TABLESPOONS FRESH LEMON JUICE
⅓ CUP ALL-PURPOSE FLOUR	2 TEASPOONS FINELY GRATED LEMON ZEST
3 LARGE EGGS, SEPARATED	¼ TEASPOON SALT
2 TABLESPOONS (¼ STICK) UNSALTED BUTTER, ROOM TEMPERATURE	¼ TEASPOON CREAM OF TARTAR
1 CUP FAT-FREE MILK	2 CUPS FRESH RASPBERRIES

Preheat oven to 350°F. Spray six 6-ounce ramekins with nonstick cooking spray. Place the ramekins in a large baking dish.

In a medium bowl whisk the sugar and flour. In another medium bowl whisk the egg yolks and butter until well blended. Whisk in the milk, lemon juice, lemon zest, and salt. Whisk the lemon mixture into the sugar mixture until blended and smooth.

In a medium bowl beat the egg whites and cream of tartar with an electric mixer at medium speed until soft peaks form. Increase speed to high and continue beating until stiff peaks form. Gently stir one-fourth of the egg white mixture into lemon mixture, then gently fold in the remaining egg white mixture.

Spoon batter into the prepared ramekins. Add hot water to baking dish to a depth of ¾ inch.

Bake 30–35 minutes or until cakes are puffy and golden on top. Using tongs, transfer the ramekins to a rack to cool for 20 minutes. Serve the cakes in the ramekins or run a knife around the edge of each cake and unmold onto plates. Serve warm or at room temperature with the berries. **Makes 6 servings.**

NUTRITION PER SERVING (1 CAKE AND ⅓ CUP BERRIES):
CALORIES 230; FAT 6.9G (SAT 2.9G, MONO 2.7G, POLY .67G);
PROTEIN 5.8G; CHOLESTEROL 117.3MG; CARBOHYDRATE 37.4G.

Cook's Note: The lemon pudding cakes can be cooled and refrigerated for up to 2 days. Let stand at room temperature at least 30 minutes before serving.

ONE-BOWL

Chocolate Chipotle Cake

A dash of cinnamon and a hint of smoky chipotle chile powder add sweet and spicy notes to this delectable, deep-chocolate cake.

NONSTICK BAKING SPRAY WITH FLOUR	1 TEASPOON GROUND CINNAMON
5 TABLESPOONS UNSALTED BUTTER, MELTED	½ TEASPOON CHIPOTLE CHILE POWDER
½ CUP UNSWEETENED COCOA POWDER (NOT DUTCH PROCESS)	¼ TEASPOON SALT
	¾ CUP WHOLE WHEAT PASTRY FLOUR (OR ALL-PURPOSE FLOUR)
1 CUP (PACKED) DARK BROWN SUGAR	
2 LARGE EGGS	½ CUP HOT WATER
½ TEASPOON BAKING SODA	⅓ CUP FAT-FREE CHOCOLATE FUDGE ICE CREAM TOPPING
1½ TEASPOONS VANILLA EXTRACT	

Preheat oven to 350°F. Spray an 8-inch round pan with nonstick baking spray with flour.

In a large bowl whisk the melted butter, cocoa powder, and brown sugar until well blended. Whisk in the eggs, one at a time, until blended and smooth. Stir in the baking soda, vanilla, cinnamon, chile powder, and salt.

Gradually add the flour to the bowl, stirring just until blended (do not overstir). Add hot water to mixture, stirring just until blended. Pour batter into the prepared pan.

Bake 22–25 minutes or until a wooden pick inserted in the center comes out clean. Cool 10 minutes on a wire rack. Cut into wedges. Warm the chocolate fudge sauce in a microwave for 15 seconds. Drizzle the chocolate sauce over cake wedges. Serve warm or at room temperature. **Makes 9 servings.**

NUTRITION PER SERVING (1 WEDGE):
CALORIES 245; FAT 8.2G (SAT 4.0G, MONO 3.4G, POLY .45G);
PROTEIN 3.7G; CHOLESTEROL 64.9MG; CARBOHYDRATE 42.3G.

Vanilla-Buttermilk Cake

WITH STRAWBERRIES

This is one of my go-to recipes; it is one of those rare recipes that manages to please all of the people all of the time. I almost always have the ingredients on hand, which means it can be thrown together in a moment's notice, and the fruit accompaniment can be whatever is in season, whether strawberries, peaches, fresh figs, or pears.

	NONSTICK BAKING SPRAY WITH FLOUR	1	CUP CAKE FLOUR
¼	CUP (½ STICK) UNSALTED BUTTER, ROOM TEMPERATURE	1	TEASPOON BAKING POWDER
⅓	CUP PLUS 1 TABLESPOON SUGAR, DIVIDED USE	½	TEASPOON BAKING SODA
		¼	TEASPOON SALT
		⅔	CUP LOW-FAT BUTTERMILK
1	LARGE EGG	1	TABLESPOON POWDERED SUGAR
1½	TEASPOONS VANILLA EXTRACT	4	CUPS SLICED STRAWBERRIES

Preheat oven to 350°F. Spray an 8-inch round cake pan with nonstick baking spray with flour.

In a large bowl beat the butter and ⅓ cup sugar with an electric mixer at medium speed until well blended (about 3 minutes). Add egg and vanilla, beating well.

In a small bowl whisk the flour, baking powder, baking soda, and salt. Add flour mixture to butter mixture alternately with buttermilk, beginning and ending with flour mixture. Pour batter into the prepared pan.

Bake 21–23 minutes or until a wooden pick inserted in the center comes out clean. Transfer cake to a cooling rack and cool in pan 10 minutes. Remove cake from pan and cool completely on rack. Sift top of cake with powdered sugar.

Combine strawberries and the remaining 1 tablespoon sugar; toss to coat. Let stand 15 minutes. Serve strawberry mixture with cake. **Makes 8 servings.**

NUTRITION PER SERVING (1 CAKE SLICE AND ½ CUP BERRY MIXTURE):
CALORIES 189; FAT 7.5G (SAT 3.5G, MONO 2.9G, POLY .48G);
PROTEIN 3.3G; CHOLESTEROL 44.2MG; CARBOHYDRATE 28.1G.

Chocolate Fudge Brownie Cake

Wonderful for anytime, any occasion, this fudgy, dense, delicious treat—part cake, part brownie—falls into the "most requested" category.

NONSTICK BAKING SPRAY WITH FLOUR

2 1-OUNCE SQUARES UNSWEETENED CHOCO-
LATE, CHOPPED

1 CUP WHOLE WHEAT PASTRY FLOUR (OR
ALL-PURPOSE FLOUR)

1 CUP PACKED LIGHT BROWN SUGAR

½ CUP UNSWEETENED COCOA POWDER (NOT
DUTCH PROCESS)

1 TEASPOON BAKING POWDER

½ TEASPOON SALT

2 LARGE EGGS

2 LARGE EGG WHITES

¾ CUP UNSWEETENED APPLESAUCE

½ CUP CANOLA OIL

2 TEASPOONS VANILLA EXTRACT

2 TEASPOONS ESPRESSO POWDER

1 TABLESPOON POWDERED SUGAR

Preheat oven to 350°F. Spray a 9-inch springform pan with nonstick baking spray with flour.

Stir the chocolate in the top of a double boiler set over simmering water until melted. Remove from heat and cool slightly.

In a medium bowl whisk the flour, brown sugar, cocoa, baking powder, and salt. In a large bowl whisk the eggs, egg whites, applesauce, canola oil, vanilla, espresso powder, and melted chocolate until blended. Sift flour mixture over. Gently fold flour into batter (do not overstir). Pour batter into the prepared pan.

Bake 33–35 minutes or until a wooden pick inserted in the center comes out clean. Transfer cake to a cooling rack and cool completely. Release the pan sides from the cake and sift powdered sugar over the cake. **Makes 12 servings.**

NUTRITION PER SERVING (1 SLICE):
CALORIES 247; FAT 12.9G (SAT 2.7G, MONO 6.6G, POLY 2.9G);
PROTEIN 4.2G; CHOLESTEROL 35.3MG; CARBOHYDRATE 32.3G.

Sticky Toffee Pudding Cake

Pudding is an English term for dessert; this recipe is an enlightened adaptation of the famous sticky toffee pudding Brits know and love. In American terms it is really a vanilla-flavored date cake, draped with a buttery brown sugar sauce. The ease of its assembly contributes to its popularity with one and all. Leftover cake (good luck with that) is excellent served plain with tea or coffee.

¾ CUP (PACKED) DARK BROWN SUGAR	½ CUP 1% LOW-FAT MILK
1⅓ CUPS WHOLE WHEAT PASTRY FLOUR (OR	2 TABLESPOONS (¼ STICK) UNSALTED
ALL-PURPOSE FLOUR), DIVIDED USE	BUTTER, MELTED
¾ CUP SUGAR	1½ TEASPOONS VANILLA EXTRACT
⅓ CUP FINELY CHOPPED PITTED DATES	1¾ CUPS BOILING WATER
1 TABLESPOON BAKING POWDER	OPTIONAL: REDUCE- FAT FROZEN WHIPPED
¼ TEASPOON SALT	TOPPING, THAWED

Preheat oven to 350°F. Spray an 8-inch square baking pan with nonstick cooking spray.

In a small bowl whisk the brown sugar and 1 tablespoon of the flour. In a medium bowl whisk the remaining flour, sugar, dates, baking powder, and salt. Make a well in the center of flour mixture. In a small bowl combine the milk, butter, and vanilla. Add to well in flour mixture, stirring just until moist.

Spread batter into the prepared pan and sprinkle with brown sugar mixture. Pour boiling water over batter (do not stir).

Bake 33–36 minutes or until the pudding is bubbly and cake springs back when touched lightly in the center. Serve warm with the whipped topping, if desired. **Makes 8 servings.**

NUTRITION PER SERVING (1 PIECE):
CALORIES 283; FAT 3.4G (SAT 1.7G, MONO 1.3G, POLY .2G);
PROTEIN 2.9G; CHOLESTEROL 8.8MG; CARBOHYDRATE 61.8G.

Black-and-Tan Marble Cake

This very American made-from-scratch cake, which is truly fast and easy, always gets rave reviews from kids and adults alike (is there anyone who doesn't like brown sugar, butter, and chocolate, especially in marbled combination?). It keeps particularly well, too—perfect for late-night pantry raids.

NONSTICK BAKING SPRAY WITH FLOUR

6 TABLESPOONS (¾ STICK) UNSALTED BUTTER, MELTED

1 CUP PACKED DARK BROWN SUGAR

2 TEASPOONS VANILLA EXTRACT

4 LARGE EGG WHITES

¾ CUP LOW-FAT BUTTERMILK

½ TEASPOON SALT

½ TEASPOON BAKING SODA

1½ CUPS WHOLE WHEAT PASTRY FLOUR (OR ALL-PURPOSE FLOUR)

3 TABLESPOONS UNSWEETENED COCOA POWDER (NOT DUTCH PROCESS)

½ TEASPOON ALMOND EXTRACT

Preheat oven to 350°F. Spray an 8-inch square baking pan with nonstick cooking spray with flour.

In a large bowl whisk the melted butter, brown sugar, and vanilla until blended. Whisk in the egg whites until blended, then whisk in the buttermilk, salt, and baking soda. Add the flour, stirring just until blended (do not overstir).

Spread half the batter into the prepared pan. Whisk the cocoa powder and almond extract into the remaining batter until blended. Spoon the chocolate batter in large spoonfuls over the batter in pan. Marble the batters with the tip of a knife.

Bake 28–30 minutes or until a wooden pick inserted in the center comes out clean. Transfer cake to a cooling rack and cool completely. **Makes 9 servings.**

NUTRITION PER SERVING (1 PIECE):
CALORIES 265; FAT 8.9G (SAT 4.5G, MONO 3.6G, POLY .39G);
PROTEIN 4.7G; CHOLESTEROL 23.1MG; CARBOHYDRATE 42.9G.

Texas Sheet Cake

Texas sheet cake is a brownie-like cake, only one-inch thick and often baked on a cookie sheet, as it is here. Food historians have not quite determined its true history, but Texans are likely to contend that the eponym comes from the cake's great big chocolate taste and richness. Whatever its origin, it is an ideal cake for family events and is always a hit at big parties, club meetings, and kid-related events.

NONSTICK BAKING SPRAY WITH FLOUR

1 CUP ALL-PURPOSE FLOUR

1 CUP WHOLE WHEAT PASTRY FLOUR (OR ALL-PURPOSE FLOUR)

2 CUPS SUGAR

1 TEASPOON BAKING SODA

½ TEASPOON GROUND CINNAMON

¼ TEASPOON SALT

¾ CUP WATER

½ CUP PLUS 6 TABLESPOONS (1¾ STICKS) BUTTER, DIVIDED USE

½ CUP UNSWEETENED COCOA POWDER (NOT DUTCH PROCESS), DIVIDED USE

½ CUP LOW-FAT BUTTERMILK

3 TEASPOONS VANILLA EXTRACT, DIVIDED USE

2 LARGE EGGS

⅓ CUP FAT-FREE MILK

3 CUPS POWDERED SUGAR

OPTIONAL: ¼ CUP CHOPPED PECANS, TOASTED

Preheat oven to 375°F. Spray a 15x10-inch jelly-roll pan with nonstick baking spray with flour.

In a large bowl whisk the flours, sugar, baking soda, cinnamon, and salt.

Combine the water, ½ cup butter, and ¼ cup cocoa powder in a small saucepan. Bring mixture to a boil, stirring frequently. Remove from heat and pour into flour mixture. Beat at medium speed with an electric mixer until well blended. Add the buttermilk, 1 teaspoon vanilla, and eggs, beating well. Pour batter into the prepared pan.

Bake 16–18 minutes or until a wooden pick inserted in the center comes out clean. Transfer pan to a cooling rack.

While the cake is baking, in a medium saucepan combine the milk, remaining 6 tablespoons butter, and remaining ¼ cup cocoa powder. Bring mixture to a boil, stirring constantly. Remove from heat, and gradually stir in powdered sugar, remaining 2 teaspoons vanilla and (optional) pecans. Spread mixture over hot cake. Cool completely on rack. Cut into squares. **Makes 20 servings.**

Cook's Note: The cake may also be made in a 13x9-inch baking pan. Bake for 20–22 minutes.

NUTRITION PER SERVING (1 SQUARE):
CALORIES 288; FAT 9.6G (SAT 4.7G, MONO 3.8G, POLY 0.4G); PROTEIN 2.8G; CHOLESTEROL 44.3MG; CARBOHYDRATE 49.9G.

Guinness Gingerbread

Moist, dark and fragrant, this gingerbread is a seasonal classic. Dark, stout beer (preferably Guinness, but any variety of stout will do) takes the place of traditional water or coffee in the recipe, adding richness and underscoring the panoply of spices. Dress it up or down, it's delectable any way you serve it.

NONSTICK BAKING SPRAY WITH FLOUR

1 CUP ALL-PURPOSE FLOUR

1 CUP WHOLE WHEAT PASTRY FLOUR (OR ALL-PURPOSE FLOUR)

1 TABLESPOON GROUND GINGER

1 TEASPOON BAKING SODA

1 TEASPOON GROUND CINNAMON

¼ TEASPOON SALT

¼ TEASPOON GROUND CLOVES

¼ TEASPOON GROUND NUTMEG

⅛ TEASPOON GROUND CARDAMOM

¾ CUP PACKED DARK BROWN SUGAR

¼ CUP (½ STICK) UNSALTED BUTTER, ROOM TEMPERATURE

3 TABLESPOONS CANOLA OIL

1 LARGE EGG

1 LARGE EGG WHITE

⅓ CUP DARK MOLASSES

1 TABLESPOON MINCED PEELED FRESH GINGER

1 CUP GUINNESS OR OTHER STOUT BEER

1 TABLESPOON POWDERED SUGAR

Preheat oven to 350°F. Spray a 9-inch round cake pan (with 2-inch high sides) with nonstick baking spray with flour.

In a medium bowl whisk the flours, ground ginger, baking soda, cinnamon, salt, cloves, nutmeg and cardamom.

In a large bowl beat the brown sugar, butter and canola oil with an electric mixer at medium speed until well blended. Add the egg and egg white, beating until blended. Beat in molasses and fresh ginger. Add flour mixture and beer alternately to brown sugar mixture, beginning and ending with flour mixture. Pour batter into the prepared pan.

Bake at 38–42 minutes or until a wooden pick inserted into the center comes out clean. Cool in pan 10 minutes on a wire rack; remove from pan. Cool completely on wire rack. Sift powdered sugar over cake. **Makes 12 servings.**

NUTRITION PER SERVING (1 SLICE):
CALORIES 238; FAT 8.1G (SAT 2.4G, MONO 3.9G, POLY 1.3G);
PROTEIN 3.0G; CHOLESTEROL 28.4MG; CARBOHYDRATE 37.5G.

Bittersweet Chocolate Ganache Cake

This impressive dessert features two classic components: a rich chocolate cake and an even richer chocolate frosting known as ganache. No one will believe it's light, nor that it's a snap to prepare—but they may very likely declare you a master of chocolate.

NONSTICK BAKING SPRAY WITH FLOUR	½ CUP WATER
1¼ CUPS CAKE FLOUR	¼ CUP (½ STICK) UNSALTED BUTTER
½ CUP UNSWEETENED COCOA POWDER (NOT DUTCH PROCESS)	1 CUP FAT-FREE BUTTERMILK
1 TEASPOON BAKING SODA	1 TABLESPOON VANILLA EXTRACT
1½ CUPS SUGAR	2 LARGE EGGS
½ OUNCE UNSWEETENED CHOCOLATE, COARSELY CHOPPED	1 LARGE EGG WHITE
	1 RECIPE BITTERSWEET CHOCOLATE GANACHE (SEE PAGE 165)

Preheat oven to 350°F. Spray a 9-inch round cake pan (with 2-inch high sides) with nonstick baking spray with flour.

In a medium bowl whisk the flour, cocoa powder, and baking soda.

In a small saucepan, combine the sugar, unsweetened chocolate, and water. Cook over moderate heat, stirring occasionally, until the sugar dissolves and the chocolate melts, about 4 minutes. Transfer the mixture to a large bowl, add the butter, and whisk until melted. Whisk in the buttermilk, vanilla, eggs, and egg white. Stir in the flour mixture until just blended (do not overstir). Pour batter into the prepared pan.

Bake 33–35 minutes or until a wooden pick inserted into the center comes out clean. Cool in pan 20 minutes on a wire rack; remove from pan. Cool completely on wire rack. Prepare Bittersweet Chocolate Ganache. Spread ganache evenly over top of cake, letting it drip down the sides. Chill 20 minutes or until set. **Makes 12 servings.**

NUTRITION PER SERVING (1 SLICE):
CALORIES 276; FAT 9.5G (SAT 5.0G, MONO 3.5G, POLY 0.4G);
PROTEIN 4.8G; CHOLESTEROL 49.1MG; CARBOHYDRATE 47.3G.

Banana Cake

WITH BUTTERSCOTCH ICING

I am particularly taken with banana cakes and breads of all shapes and varieties, largely for their homespun flavor and lack of pretense. This version is no exception—it gets a double dose of banana, mashed and stirred into the batter and also diced and folded in. It's a perfect cake for picnics and packing in lunchbags, in particular.

NONSTICK BAKING SPRAY WITH FLOUR

¼ CUP (½ STICK) UNSALTED BUTTER, ROOM TEMPERATURE

¾ CUP PACKED LIGHT BROWN SUGAR

2 LARGE EGGS

2 LARGE EGG WHITES

½ CUP LOW-FAT BUTTERMILK

1 CUP MASHED BANANA (ABOUT 2 LARGE OVERRIPE BANANAS)

1 LARGE RIPE BANANA, PEELED AND DICED INTO ¼-INCH CHUNKS

2 TABLESPOONS FRESH LEMON JUICE

2 CUPS WHOLE WHEAT PASTRY FLOUR

1½ TEASPOONS BAKING SODA

½ TEASPOON GRATED NUTMEG

1 RECIPE BUTTERSCOTCH ICING (SEE PAGE 158)

Preheat oven to 350°F. Spray a 9-inch square baking pan with nonstick baking spray with flour.

In a large bowl beat the butter and brown sugar with an electric mixer at medium speed until well blended (about 5 minutes). Add the eggs and egg whites, one at a time, beating well after each addition. Beat in the buttermilk until blended.

In a medium bowl combine the mashed bananas, diced bananas, and lemon juice. In a small bowl whisk the flour, baking soda, and nutmeg. Fold the banana mixture into the butter mixture, then fold in the flour mixture until just blended (do not overmix). Pour batter into the prepared pan.

Bake 30–34 minutes or until a wooden pick inserted in the center comes out clean. Transfer cake to wire rack and cool 15 minutes. Prepare Butterscotch Icing. Pour icing over cake and let stand 20 minutes. Cut into 10 pieces. Serve warm or cool to room temperature. **Makes 10 servings.**

NUTRITION PER SERVING (1 PIECE):
CALORIES 273; FAT 8.8G (SAT 4.2G, MONO 3.5G, POLY 0.5G);
PROTEIN 5.4G; CHOLESTEROL 62.6MG; CARBOHYDRATE 43.8G.

Mini Chocolate Lava Cakes

I had my first (unforgettable) taste of chocolate lava cake—also known as molten chocolate cake—sometime back in the late nineties. Now a classic offering on dessert menus across the country, it's also a wonderful option to make at home. Here I've lightened the fat and calories, but none of the rich chocolate taste. Most important, the filling for these luscious little cakes still has the all-important "ooze" factor.

4 OUNCES BITTERSWEET CHOCOLATE, COARSELY CHOPPED	2 TABLESPOONS CANOLA OIL
2½ TABLESPOONS UNSALTED BUTTER, CUT INTO CHUNKS	1 TEASPOON VANILLA EXTRACT
1 TABLESPOON SUGAR	⅛ TEASPOON SALT
1½ TABLESPOONS FAT-FREE MILK	3 TABLESPOONS ALL-PURPOSE FLOUR
2 TEASPOONS INSTANT ESPRESSO POWDER, DIVIDED USE	1 TABLESPOON UNSWEETENED COCOA POWDER (NOT DUTCH PROCESS)
1 TABLESPOON HONEY	6 TABLESPOONS POWDERED SUGAR, DIVIDED USE
1 LARGE EGG	6 SMALL MINT SPRIGS FOR GARNISH

Place the chocolate and butter in a medium microwave-safe bowl. Microwave on HIGH 1 minute. Stir, then continue microwaving on medium, stirring every 20 seconds, until chocolate melts completely. Set aside.

In a small microwave-safe bowl whisk the sugar, milk, and 1 teaspoon espresso powder. Microwave on HIGH for 20 seconds. Stir until the sugar dissolves. Whisk in the honey and half the melted chocolate (reserve the other half for the batter) until completely smooth. Cover and freezer until cold and firm, about 30 minutes.

Once the filling has chilled for 20 minutes, preheat the oven to 350°F. Spray 6 cups of a standard-size muffin pan with nonstick cooking spray.

In a medium bowl whisk the egg, canola oil, vanilla, salt, and the remaining 1 teaspoon espresso powder until smooth. Return the remaining chocolate mixture to the microwave. Microwave on MEDIUM, stirring every 20 seconds, until just warm again (do not overheat). In two batches, whisk the egg mixture into the warm chocolate until well blended. Sift the flour, cocoa powder, and 5 tablespoons powdered sugar over the batter and whisk until just blended.

Remove the filling from the freezer. Spoon half the batter into the prepared muffin cups, about 2 rounded teaspoons per cup. Divide the filling onto the center of each.

Divide the remaining batter evenly among the muffin cups, about 2 rounded teaspoons per cake. Smooth out the batter to cover the filling.

Bake 9–10 minutes until the edges look dry and puffed but the centers still look very underdone and pudding-like. Transfer muffin pan to a wire rack and cool 2 minutes. Run a knife around the edge of each cake. Place a cutting board on top of the pan and invert the cakes onto it. Serve the warm cakes, sprinkled with remaining tablespoon powdered sugar and garnished with a mint sprig. **Makes 6 servings.**

NUTRITION PER SERVING (1 MINI CAKE):
CALORIES 254; FAT 16.3G (SAT 6.6G, MONO 7.0G, POLY 1.8G);
PROTEIN 2.6G; CHOLESTEROL 48.8MG; CARBOHYDRATE 28.4G.

2. BUNDT

Bliss

SOUR CREAM POUND **CAKE**, TRIPLE-LEMON BUTTERMILK POUND **CAKE**, CINNAMON GRAHAM BUNDT **CAKE**, PEAR POUND **CAKE** WITH HONEY GLAZE, BANANA-RUM BUNDT **CAKE**, CHOCOLATE BOURBON **CAKE**, PB&J BUNDT **CAKE**, CITRUS-SCENTED OLIVE OIL **CAKE**, CARAMEL APPLE BUNDT **CAKE**, DOUBLE-CHOCOLATE BUNDT **CAKE**, BLUEBERRY BUNDT **CAKE**, IRISH CREAM POUND **CAKE**, FRESH LIME POUND **CAKE**, CRANBERRY BUNDT **CAKE**, SOUR CREAM STREUSEL COFFEE **CAKE**, POLENTA POUND **CAKE**, TART CHERRY—ALMOND POUND **CAKE**, GRAND MARNIER-GLAZED ORANGE POUND **CAKE**, RUM RAISIN POUND **CAKE**, PUMPKIN POUND CAKE, CHARLOTTE'S SHERRY POUND **CAKE**, CARROT **CAKE** BUNDT . . .

Sour Cream Pound Cake

This luscious pound cake is not as rich as the traditional version, but it is just as (or, perhaps, more) delicious. I love to nibble on a thin slice mid afternoon, with a cup of tea, but I also find it a perfect option for entertaining: make it ahead and dish it up with steaming cups of espresso or slice, plate, and pile it high with seasonal fresh fruit.

NONSTICK BAKING SPRAY WITH FLOUR	1 CUP REDUCED-FAT SOUR CREAM
3 CUPS SUGAR	½ CUP NONFAT YOGURT
¾ CUP (1½ STICKS) UNSALTED BUTTER, ROOM TEMPERATURE	2 TEASPOONS VANILLA EXTRACT
	1 TEASPOON BAKING SODA
7 LARGE EGG WHITES, ROOM TEMPERATURE	4½ CUPS SIFTED CAKE FLOUR
1 LARGE EGG, ROOM TEMPERATURE	¼ TEASPOON SALT

Preheat oven to 325°F. Spray a 12-cup Bundt pan with nonstick baking spray with flour.

In a large cream beat the sugar and butter with an electric mixer at medium speed until well blended (about 5 minutes). Add egg whites and egg, one at a time, beating well after each addition.

In a small bowl whisk the sour cream, yogurt, vanilla, and baking soda until blended. Set aside. In a medium bowl whisk the flour and salt. Add flour mixture to butter mixture alternately with sour cream mixture, beginning and ending with flour mixture. Pour batter into prepared pan.

Bake 1 hour and 35 minutes or until a wooden pick inserted in the center comes out clean. Transfer cake to a cooling rack and cool in pan 10 minutes. Remove cake from pan and cool completely on rack. **Makes 24 servings.**

Variations
Almond Pound Cake: Add 1 teaspoon almond extract, and decrease vanilla to 1 teaspoon.
Brown Sugar Pound Cake: Add 2 cups firmly packed dark brown sugar and decrease sugar to 1 cup.
Citrus Pound Cake: Add 1 tablespoon freshly grated citrus zest (e.g., lemon, lime, tangerine, orange), and decrease vanilla to ½ teaspoon.
Cook's Note: To freeze any extra pound cake, first cool the cake completely on a wire rack (do not glaze). Cut into individual slices and place in a heavy-duty zip-top plastic bag. Remove excess air from the bag; then seal and place it in the freezer for up to four months. To thaw, let cake stand at room temperature.

NUTRITION PER SERVING (1 SLICE):
CALORIES 247; FAT 7.7G (SAT 3.9G, MONO 2.9G, POLY 0.4G);
PROTEIN 3.3G; CHOLESTEROL 28.9MG; CARBOHYDRATE 41.9G.

TRIPLE-LEMON BUTTERMILK

Pound Cake

In each delicious bite you'll get the fresh flavor of lemon, times three, blended into a buttery batter. It's a perfect summertime cake.

NONSTICK BAKING SPRAY WITH FLOUR

3¼ CUPS ALL-PURPOSE FLOUR

½ TEASPOON BAKING SODA

¼ TEASPOON SALT

¾ CUP (1½ STICKS) UNSALTED BUTTER, ROOM TEMPERATURE

2½ CUPS SUGAR

2 TEASPOONS LEMON EXTRACT

3 LARGE EGGS

1½ TABLESPOONS GRATED LEMON ZEST

4 TABLESPOONS FRESH LEMON JUICE, DIVIDED USE

1 CUP LOW-FAT BUTTERMILK, WELL-SHAKEN

1 CUP POWDERED SUGAR

Preheat oven to 325°F. Spray a 12-cup Bundt pan with nonstick baking spray with flour.

In a medium bowl whisk the flour, baking soda, and salt.

In a large bowl beat the butter with an electric mixer at medium speed until light and fluffy. Gradually add the sugar and lemon extract, beating until well blended. Add the eggs, one at a time, beating well after each addition. Add the lemon zest and 2 tablespoons lemon juice, then beat 30 seconds.

Add flour mixture to sugar mixture alternately with the buttermilk, beating at low speed, beginning and ending with the flour mixture. Spoon batter into the prepared pan.

Bake 1 hour and 10 minutes or until a wooden pick inserted in the center comes out clean. Transfer cake to a cooling rack and cool in pan 10 minutes. Remove cake from pan and cool completely on rack. In a small cup combine the powdered sugar and remaining 2 tablespoons of lemon juice until blended. Drizzle or brush glaze over the top of the cake. **Makes 20 servings.**

Variation

Lemon Poppy Seed Pound Cake: Prepare as directed above, but add ⅓ cup poppy seeds with the flour mixture.

NUTRITION PER SERVING (1 SLICE):
CALORIES 277; FAT 8.5G (SAT 4.1G, MONO 3.4G, POLY 0.5G);
PROTEIN 3.6G; CHOLESTEROL 52.1MG; CARBOHYDRATE 47.4G.

Cinnamon Graham Bundt Cake

I loved cinnamon graham crackers a child. Thanks to my infant son's fondness for them, I've discovered that the fondness never faded. They are the inspiration for this playful cake, a taste of childhood for palates of all ages. I blend graham crackers crumbs right into the buttery batter along with ground cinnamon, brown sugar, and vanilla.

NONSTICK BAKING SPRAY WITH FLOUR

1 CUP ALL-PURPOSE FLOUR

1 CUP WHOLE WHEAT PASTRY FLOUR (OR ALL-PURPOSE FLOUR)

1⅓ CUPS LOW-FAT GRAHAM CRACKER CRUMBS (ABOUT 8 WHOLE COOKIE SHEETS)

1 TEASPOON BAKING POWDER

1 TEASPOON BAKING SODA

1¼ TEASPOONS GROUND CINNAMON

¼ TEASPOON GROUND NUTMEG

1 TEASPOON SALT

1 CUP PACKED BROWN SUGAR

½ CUP SUGAR

4 OUNCES (½ OF AN 8-OUNCE PACKAGE) FAT-FREE CREAM CHEESE

6 TABLESPOONS (¾ STICK) UNSALTED BUTTER, ROOM TEMPERATURE

2 LARGE EGGS

1 LARGE EGG WHITE

1 CUP LOW-FAT BUTTERMILK

1 TABLESPOON POWDERED SUGAR

Preheat oven to 350°F. Spray a 12-cup Bundt pan with nonstick baking spray with flour.

In a medium bowl whisk the flours, graham cracker crumbs, baking powder, baking soda, cinnamon, nutmeg, and salt.

In a large bowl beat the brown sugar, sugar, cream cheese, and butter with an electric mixer at medium speed until well blended (about 5 minutes). Add the eggs and egg white, one at a time, beating well after each addition.

Add the flour mixture to butter mixture alternately with the buttermilk, beginning and ending with the flour mixture. Pour batter into the prepared pan.

Bake 47–50 minutes or until a wooden pick inserted in the center comes out clean. Transfer cake to a cooling rack and cool in pan 5 minutes. Remove cake from pan and cool completely on rack. Sprinkle with powdered sugar. **Makes 16 servings.**

NUTRITION PER SERVING (1 SLICE):
CALORIES 181; FAT 6.1G (SAT 2.8G, MONO 2.4G, POLY 0.3G);
PROTEIN 4.8G; CHOLESTEROL 40.3MG; CARBOHYDRATE 27.1G.

Pear Pound Cake

WITH HONEY GLAZE

Dense, moist and delectable, this homey cake has a lovely balance of fall flavors. An equal amount of apple or quince can be used in place of the pears.

NONSTICK BAKING SPRAY WITH FLOUR	4 LARGE EGGS
1½ CUPS ALL-PURPOSE FLOUR	½ CUP 2% LOW-FAT MILK
1½ CUPS WHOLE WHEAT PASTRY FLOUR (OR	½ CUP CANOLA OIL
ALL-PURPOSE FLOUR)	1 TEASPOON VANILLA EXTRACT
1 TABLESPOON BAKING POWDER	2 CUPS CHOPPED PEELED PEARS (ABOUT 3
½ TEASPOON SALT	MEDIUM-LARGE PEARS)
1½ TEASPOONS GROUND CARDAMOM	¼ CUP CHOPPED WALNUTS, LIGHTLY TOASTED
1 CUP SUGAR	⅓ CUP HONEY
¾ CUP PACKED LIGHT BROWN SUGAR	2 TABLESPOONS FRESH LEMON JUICE

Preheat oven to 350°F. Spray a 12-cup Bundt pan with nonstick baking spray with flour.

In a medium bowl whisk the flours, baking powder, salt, and cardamom.

In a large bowl beat the sugar, brown sugar, and eggs with an electric mixer at medium speed until thick and pale (about 3 minutes). In a small bowl combine the milk, canola oil, and vanilla.

Add the flour mixture to the egg mixture alternately with the milk mixture, beginning and ending with flour mixture. Fold in pears and walnuts. Pour batter into the prepared pan.

Bake 50–55 minutes or until a wooden pick inserted in the center comes out clean. Transfer cake to a cooling rack and cool in pan 15 minutes. Remove cake from pan.

To prepare glaze, combine honey and lemon juice in a small saucepan over medium heat. Cook 2 minutes, stirring constantly. Brush warm glaze over top and sides of cake. Cool cake completely on rack. **Makes 18 servings.**

NUTRITION PER SERVING (1 SLICE):
CALORIES 269; FAT 8.6G (SAT 0.9G, MONO 4.2G, POLY 2.8G);
PROTEIN 4.1G; CHOLESTEROL 47.5MG; CARBOHYDRATE 44.9G.

Banana-Rum Bundt Cake

The inspiration for this cake comes from the Caribbean, where both bananas and rum are popular ingredients in a wide range of both sweet and savory dishes. Here the two ingredients coalesce in sweet harmony—good luck resisting a second helping.

NONSTICK BAKING SPRAY WITH FLOUR

1½ CUPS ALL-PURPOSE FLOUR

1 CUP WHOLE WHEAT PASTRY FLOUR (OR ALL-PURPOSE FLOUR)

2 TEASPOONS BAKING POWDER

1 TEASPOON BAKING SODA

1 TEASPOON GROUND CINNAMON

¼ TEASPOON SALT

1 CUP MASHED RIPE BANANA

⅓ CUP PLAIN NONFAT YOGURT

4 TABLESPOONS DARK RUM, DIVIDED USE

1 TABLESPOON VANILLA EXTRACT

⅔ CUP UNSALTED BUTTER, ROOM TEMPERATURE

1¾ CUPS PACKED LIGHT BROWN SUGAR

4 LARGE EGG WHITES

1 LARGE EGG

1 CUP SIFTED POWDERED SUGAR

1 TABLESPOON UNSALTED BUTTER, MELTED

Preheat oven to 350°F. Spray a 12-cup Bundt pan with nonstick baking spray with flour.

In a medium bowl whisk the flours, baking powder, baking soda, cinnamon, and salt. Set aside. In a small bowl combine the banana, yogurt, 2 tablespoons rum, and vanilla.

In a large bowl beat the butter with an electric mixer at medium speed until light and fluffy. Gradually add the brown sugar, beating until well blended. Add the egg whites and egg, one at a time, beating well after each addition.

Add the flour mixture to the sugar mixture alternately with the banana mixture, beating at low speed, beginning and ending with flour mixture. Spoon batter into prepared pan.

Bake 1 hour or until a wooden pick inserted in the center comes out clean. Transfer cake to a cooling rack and cool in pan 10 minutes. Remove cake from pan and cool completely on rack. In a small cup combine the powdered sugar, melted butter, and remaining 2 tablespoons rum until blended. Brush or drizzle glaze over top of cake. **Makes 16 servings.**

NUTRITION PER SERVING (1 SLICE):
CALORIES 297; FAT 9.5G (SAT 4.6G, MONO 3.8G, POLY 0.5G);
PROTEIN 3.7; CHOLESTEROL 36.9MG; CARBOHYDRATE 48.5G.

Chocolate Bourbon Cake

A perfect combination of cocoa, chopped chocolate and bourbon, this is a dessert experience for those who welcome the true essence of chocolate—with a spike of grown-up flair.

NONSTICK BAKING SPRAY WITH FLOUR

2 CUPS ALL-PURPOSE FLOUR

1 CUP UNSWEETENED COCOA POWDER (NOT DUTCH PROCESS)

1 TABLESPOON INSTANT ESPRESSO POWDER

1 TEASPOON BAKING SODA

½ TEASPOON SALT

½ CUP 2% LOW-FAT MILK

½ CUP BOURBON (OR WHISKEY)

2 TEASPOONS VANILLA

6 TABLESPOONS (¾ STICK) UNSALTED BUTTER, SOFTENED

2 TABLESPOONS CANOLA OIL

2 CUPS SUGAR

3 LARGE EGGS

2 LARGE EGG WHITES

2 OUNCES BITTERSWEET CHOCOLATE, FINELY CHOPPED

Preheat oven to 350°F. Spray a 12-cup Bundt pan with nonstick baking spray with flour.

In a medium bowl whisk the flour, cocoa powder, espresso powder, baking soda, and salt. In a small bowl combine the milk, bourbon, and vanilla.

In a large bowl beat the butter, canola oil, and sugar with an electric mixer at medium speed until light and fluffy. Add the eggs and egg whites, one at a time, beating well after each addition.

Add the flour mixture to the butter mixture alternately with milk mixture, beating at low speed, beginning and ending with the flour mixture. Fold in the chocolate. Spoon batter into the prepared pan.

Bake 50–55 minutes or until a wooden pick inserted in the center comes out clean. Transfer cake to a cooling rack and cool in pan 10 minutes. Remove cake from pan and cool completely on rack. **Makes 16 servings.**

NUTRITION PER SERVING (1 SLICE):
CALORIES 273; FAT 9.3G (SAT 3.8G, MONO 3.9G, POLY 0.9G);
PROTEIN 4.6G; CHOLESTEROL 52.4MG; CARBOHYDRATE 42.4G.

PB and J Bundt Cake

I know that I am not alone in thinking that anytime is a good time for a peanut butter and jelly sandwich. Now I can have it in cake form, and still without an excess of fat and calories. I start with a brown sugar and butter pound cake, then layer in creamy peanut butter, chopped peanuts and a tangy raspberry ribbon.

NONSTICK BAKING SPRAY WITH FLOUR

¾ CUP PACKED LIGHT BROWN SUGAR

¾ CUP SUGAR

½ CUP (1 STICK) BUTTER, ROOM TEMPERA-
   TURE

2 LARGE EGGS

1 16-OUNCE CONTAINER FAT-FREE SOUR
   CREAM

1 TEASPOON VANILLA EXTRACT

1¼ CUPS ALL-PURPOSE FLOUR

1¼ CUPS WHOLE WHEAT PASTRY FLOUR (OR
   ALL-PURPOSE FLOUR)

1 TEASPOON BAKING POWDER

½ TEASPOON BAKING SODA

¼ TEASPOON SALT

¼ CUP CHOPPED ROASTED PEANUTS

2 TABLESPOONS REDUCED-FAT CREAMY
   PEANUT BUTTER

2 TABLESPOONS SEEDLESS RASPBERRY JAM,
   STIRRED TO LOOSEN

1 TABLESPOON POWDERED SUGAR

Preheat oven to 350°F. Spray a 12-cup Bundt pan with nonstick baking spray with flour.

In a large bowl beat the sugars and butter with an electric mixer at medium speed until well blended (about 5 minutes). Add the eggs, one at a time, beating well after each addition.

In a small bowl whisk the sour cream and vanilla until blended. In a medium bowl whisk the flours, baking powder, baking soda, and salt. Add the flour mixture to the butter mixture alternately with the sour cream mixture, beginning and ending with the flour mixture.

Spoon half the batter into the prepared pan, sprinkle evenly with peanuts. Drop small spoonfuls of peanut butter and jam over the peanuts. Spoon remaining batter over peanut butter and jam, and swirl the batter using the tip of a knife.

Bake 55 minutes or until a wooden pick inserted in the center comes out clean. Transfer cake to a cooling rack and cool in pan 15 minutes. Remove cake from pan and cool completely on rack. Sprinkle cake with powdered sugar. **Makes 16 servings.**

NUTRITION PER SERVING (1 SLICE):
CALORIES 264; FAT 8.8G (SAT 3.6G, MONO 3.7G, POLY 0.9G);
PROTEIN 4.9G; CHOLESTEROL 45.4MG; CARBOHYDRATE 42.1G.

Citrus-Scented Olive Oil Cake

This is a sophisticated, not-too-sweet cake—I cannot get enough of it, nor can my husband. You can use either extra-virgin or regular olive oil—both are delicious. Extra-virgin yields a fruitier, more pronounced olive-oil flavor; regular olive oil results in a lighter taste overall.

	NONSTICK BAKING SPRAY WITH FLOUR
2½	CUPS SUGAR
1½	CUPS FAT-FREE MILK
4	LARGE EGG WHITES
1	LARGE EGG
½	CUP OLIVE OIL
2	TABLESPOONS GRATED LEMON ZEST
3	TABLESPOONS FRESH LEMON JUICE
1¼	CUPS ALL-PURPOSE FLOUR
1	CUP WHOLE WHEAT PASTRY FLOUR (OR ALL-PURPOSE FLOUR)
1	TEASPOON BAKING POWDER
1	TEASPOON SALT
½	TEASPOON BAKING SODA
½	TEASPOON GROUND CORIANDER
¼	CUP ORANGE MARMALADE
2	TABLESPOONS POWDERED SUGAR

Preheat oven to 350°F. Spray a 12-cup Bundt pan with nonstick baking spray with flour.

In a large bowl whisk the sugar, milk, egg whites, egg, olive oil, lemon zest, and lemon juice until well blended.

In a medium bowl whisk the flours, baking powder, salt, baking soda, and coriander. Set aside. Whisk the flour mixture into olive oil mixture until just blended. Pour batter into the prepared pan.

Bake 50–55 minutes or until a wooden pick inserted in the center comes out clean. Transfer cake to a cooling rack and cool completely in pan. Remove cake from pan and place on rack.

Place the orange marmalade in a microwave-safe bowl. Microwave 1 minute. Stir and spoon hot marmalade evenly over cake. Cool completely. Sprinkle with powdered sugar. **Makes 16 servings.**

NUTRITION PER SERVING (1 SLICE):
CALORIES 278; FAT 7.3G (SAT 1.1G, MONO 5.1G, POLY 0.8G);
PROTEIN 3.8G; CHOLESTEROL 13.7MG; CARBOHYDRATE 50.2G.

Caramel Apple Bundt Cake

Caramel apples, all grown up in a refined cake. A homemade caramel glaze is drizzled over the top, balancing the tart-sweetness of apples for a harmony of cake, caramel, and fruit in every bite.

NONSTICK BAKING SPRAY WITH FLOUR

1 CUP WHOLE WHEAT PASTRY FLOUR (OR ALL-PURPOSE FLOUR)

1 CUP ALL-PURPOSE FLOUR

1½ TEASPOONS BAKING SODA, DIVIDED USE

1½ TEASPOONS GROUND CINNAMON

2¼ CUPS PACKED LIGHT BROWN SUGAR, DIVIDED USE

½ CUP WATER

¼ CUP (½ STICK) UNSALTED BUTTER, MELTED

¼ CUP CANOLA OIL

2½ TEASPOONS VANILLA EXTRACT, DIVIDED USE

3 LARGE EGGS, LIGHTLY BEATEN

3 CUPS CHOPPED, PEELED GOLDEN DELICIOUS APPLES

½ CUP LOW-FAT BUTTERMILK

1 TABLESPOON HONEY

Preheat oven to 350°F. Spray a 12-cup Bundt pan with nonstick baking spray with flour.

In a large bowl whisk the flours, 1 teaspoon baking soda, cinnamon, and 1½ cups brown sugar. Add the water, butter, canola oil, 2 teaspoons vanilla, and eggs. Beat with an electric mixer at medium speed until well blended (about 3 minutes). Fold in the apples. Pour batter into the prepared pan.

Bake 50–55 minutes or until a wooden pick inserted in the center comes out clean. Transfer cake to a cooling rack and cool in pan 10 minutes. Remove cake from pan and cool completely on rack.

To prepare glaze, combine the buttermilk, honey, remaining ¾ cup brown sugar, and remaining ½ teaspoon baking soda in a medium saucepan. Cook over medium heat 5–7 minutes or until sugar dissolves and mixture is light brown, stirring constantly. Stir in remaining ½ teaspoon vanilla. Pour hot glaze over cake. Cool completely. **Makes 16 servings.**

NUTRITION PER SERVING (1 SLICE):
CALORIES 257; FAT 7.7G (SAT 2.2G, MONO 3.7G, POLY 1.3G);
PROTEIN 3.2G; CHOLESTEROL 48.3MG; CARBOHYDRATE 44.9G.

Double-Chocolate Bundt Cake

This old-fashioned, chocolate-chocolate chip Bundt cake is swoon-worthy. Unsweetened natural cocoa powder—and lots of it—in combination with buttermilk, vanilla, and espresso, makes for an intensely chocolate, moist cake that gets better and better as it sits.

NONSTICK BAKING SPRAY WITH FLOUR

1¼ CUPS ALL-PURPOSE FLOUR

½ CUP WHOLE WHEAT PASTRY FLOUR (OR ALL-PURPOSE FLOUR)

2 CUPS SUGAR

¾ CUP UNSWEETENED COCOA POWDER (NOT DUTCH PROCESS)

1½ TEASPOONS BAKING SODA

1½ TEASPOONS BAKING POWDER

1 TEASPOON SALT

1 CUP BOILING WATER

1 TABLESPOON INSTANT ESPRESSO OR COFFEE POWDER

1¼ CUPS LOW-FAT BUTTERMILK

2 LARGE EGGS, LIGHTLY BEATEN

¼ CUP CANOLA OIL

2 TEASPOONS VANILLA EXTRACT

⅔ CUP MINIATURE SEMISWEET CHOCOLATE CHIPS

2 TABLESPOONS POWDERED SUGAR

Preheat oven to 350°F. Spray a 12-cup Bundt pan with nonstick baking spray with flour.

In a large bowl whisk the flours, sugar, cocoa powder, baking soda, baking powder, and salt. Combine the boiling water and espresso powder in a small cup. Add the espresso mixture, buttermilk, eggs, canola oil, and vanilla to flour mixture. Beat with an electric mixer at medium speed for 2 minutes. Stir in chocolate chips. Pour batter into the prepared pan.

Bake 45–50 minutes or until a wooden pick inserted in the center comes out clean. Transfer cake to a cooling rack and cool in pan 10 minutes. Remove cake from pan and cool completely on rack. Sprinkle with powdered sugar. **Makes 16 servings.**

NUTRITION PER SERVING (1 SLICE):
CALORIES 221; FAT 5.1G (SAT 1.0G, MONO 2.5G, POLY 1.2G);
PROTEIN 4.1G; CHOLESTEROL 27.9MG; CARBOHYDRATE 41.9G.

Blueberry Bundt Cake

This is one of my favorite ways to eat blueberries. Brushing the lemon-powdered sugar glaze onto the warm cake allows it to sink in, tenderizing the cake, adding tartness, and helping to keep the cake fresh for a few days longer than usual.

NONSTICK BAKING SPRAY WITH FLOUR	2 TEASPOONS VANILLA EXTRACT
2 CUPS SUGAR	2 CUPS FRESH BLUEBERRIES
½ CUP (1 STICK) UNSALTED BUTTER	2 CUPS ALL-PURPOSE FLOUR, DIVIDED USE
4 OUNCES (½ OF AN 8-OUNCE PACKAGE) ⅓-LESS-FAT CREAM CHEESE, ROOM TEMPERATURE	1 CUP WHOLE WHEAT PASTRY FLOUR (OR ALL-PURPOSE FLOUR)
3 LARGE EGGS	1½ TEASPOONS BAKING POWDER
1 LARGE EGG WHITE	½ TEASPOON BAKING SODA
1 CUP LOW-FAT BUTTERMILK	½ TEASPOON SALT
1 TABLESPOON GRATED LEMON ZEST	⅔ CUP POWDERED SUGAR
	1½ TABLESPOONS LEMON JUICE

Preheat oven to 325°F. Spray a 12-cup Bundt pan with nonstick baking spray with flour.

In a large bowl beat the sugar, butter, and cream cheese with an electric mixer at medium speed until well blended (about 5 minutes). Add the eggs and egg whites, one at a time, beating well after each addition.

In a small bowl whisk the buttermilk, lemon zest, and vanilla until blended.

Combine the blueberries and 2 tablespoons of the all-purpose flour in a small bowl, and toss well to coat the blueberries. In a medium bowl whisk the remaining all-purpose flour, whole wheat pastry flour, baking powder, baking soda, and salt. Add the flour mixture to the butter mixture alternately with the buttermilk mixture, beginning and ending with the flour mixture. Fold in blueberries. Pour batter into prepared pan.

Bake 1 hour and 10 minutes or until a wooden pick inserted in the center comes out clean. Transfer cake to a cooling rack and cool in the pan 10 minutes. Remove cake from pan. In a small cup combine the powdered sugar and lemon juice. Brush the glaze all over the warm cake. Cool completely on rack. **Makes 18 servings.**

NUTRITION PER SERVING (1 SLICE):
CALORIES 270; FAT 8.2G (SAT 4.1G, MONO 3.1G, POLY 0.5G);
PROTEIN 4.7G; CHOLESTEROL 55.4MG; CARBOHYDRATE 45.2G.

Irish Cream Pound Cake

The distinctive flavor of Irish cream liqueur—rich with notes of chocolate, caramel, vanilla, and whiskey—make this one gloriously delicious pound cake.

NONSTICK BAKING SPRAY WITH FLOUR

1 8-OUNCE PACKAGE FAT-FREE CREAM CHEESE, ROOM TEMPERATURE

½ CUP (1 STICK) UNSALTED BUTTER, ROOM TEMPERATURE

1¼ CUPS PACKED LIGHT BROWN SUGAR

¾ CUP SUGAR

2 TEASPOONS VANILLA EXTRACT

3 LARGE EGGS

2¾ CUPS CAKE FLOUR

1 TEASPOON BAKING POWDER

½ TEASPOON SALT

¾ CUP IRISH CREAM LIQUEUR

2 TABLESPOONS POWDERED SUGAR

Preheat oven to 350°F. Spray a 10-inch tube pan with nonstick baking spray with flour.

In a large bowl beat the cream cheese, butter, brown sugar, sugar, and vanilla with an electric mixer at medium speed until well blended (about 5 minutes). Add the eggs, one at a time, beating well after each addition.

In a medium bowl whisk the flour, baking powder, and salt. Add the flour mixture to butter mixture alternately with liqueur, beginning and ending with the flour mixture. Pour batter into the prepared pan.

Bake 50–55 minutes or until a wooden pick inserted in the center comes out clean. Transfer cake to a cooling rack and cool in pan 10 minutes. Remove cake from pan and cool completely on rack. Sprinkle with powdered sugar. **Makes 16 servings.**

NUTRITION PER SERVING (1 SLICE):
CALORIES 298; FAT 7.4G (SAT 3.5G, MONO 2.9G, POLY 0.5G);
PROTEIN 4.8G; CHOLESTEROL 56.9MG; CARBOHYDRATE 46.8G.

Fresh Lime Pound Cake

An indulgent treat any time of year, this zesty, tart-sweet cake will delight your senses with the flavor of fresh, sun-ripened limes.

NONSTICK BAKING SPRAY WITH FLOUR	2¼ CUPS ALL-PURPOSE FLOUR
10 TABLESPOONS (1¼ STICKS) UNSALTED BUTTER, ROOM TEMPERATURE	1 TEASPOON BAKING POWDER
4 OUNCES (½ OF AN 8-OUNCE PACKAGE) ⅓-LESS-FAT CREAM CHEESE, ROOM TEMPERATURE	¼ TEASPOON SALT
	½ CUP LOW-FAT BUTTERMILK
	6 TABLESPOONS FRESH LIME JUICE
1 TABLESPOON GRATED LIME ZEST	2 TEASPOONS VANILLA EXTRACT
1¾ CUPS SUGAR, DIVIDED USE	3 LARGE EGG WHITES
3 LARGE EGGS	2 TABLESPOONS POWDERED SUGAR

Preheat oven to 325°F. Spray a 10-inch tube pan with nonstick baking spray with flour.

In a large bowl beat the butter, cream cheese, lime zest, and 1½ cups of the sugar with an electric mixer at medium speed until well blended (about 5 minutes). Add the eggs, one at a time, beating well after each addition.

In a medium bowl whisk the flour, baking powder, and salt. In a small bowl whisk the buttermilk, lime juice, and vanilla. Add the flour mixture to the butter mixture alternately with the buttermilk mixture, beginning and ending with the flour mixture.

Place the egg whites in a medium bowl. Beat with an electric mixer (using clean, dry beaters) at high speed until soft peaks form. Add remaining ¼ cup sugar, 1 tablespoon at a time, beating until stiff peaks form. Gently fold one-third of the egg white mixture into the batter, then fold in remaining egg white mixture. Pour batter into the prepared pan.

Bake 1 hour and 10 minutes or until a wooden pick inserted in the center comes out clean. Transfer cake to a cooling rack and cool in pan 10 minutes. Remove cake from pan and cool completely on rack. Sprinkle with powdered sugar. **Makes 16 servings.**

NUTRITION PER SERVING (1 SLICE):
CALORIES 255; FAT 10.5G (SAT 5.3G, MONO 4.0G, POLY 0.5G);
PROTEIN 4.0G, CHOLESTEROL 65.8MG, CARBOHYDRATE 36.1G

Cranberry Bundt Cake

When the pumpkin pie is gone, but you've only just begun to get your fill of Turkey-Day desserts, this cranberry-studded Bundt cake fills the void quite nicely. Best of all, the flavors continue to develop and the cake tastes even better a few days after it's baked, so it's perfect to have on hand in late autumn-early winter, when guests tend to drop in at a moment's notice.

NONSTICK BAKING SPRAY WITH FLOUR

1⅓ CUPS ORANGE JUICE

½ CUP CANOLA OIL

1 TABLESPOON GRATED ORANGE ZEST

2 LARGE EGGS

1 TEASPOON ALMOND EXTRACT

2⅔ CUPS ALL-PURPOSE FLOUR

1⅓ CUPS WHOLE WHEAT PASTRY FLOUR (OR ALL-PURPOSE FLOUR)

2 CUPS SUGAR

2 TEASPOONS BAKING POWDER

1 TEASPOON BAKING SODA

½ TEASPOON SALT

2⅔ CUPS CHOPPED FRESH CRANBERRIES

½ CUP CHOPPED LIGHTLY TOASTED ALMONDS

Preheat oven to 325°F. Spray a 12-cup Bundt pan with nonstick baking spray with flour.

In a medium bowl whisk the orange juice, canola oil, orange zest, eggs, and almond extract until blended.

In a large bowl whisk the flours, sugar, baking powder, baking soda, and salt. Make a well in the center of the flour mixture. Add the orange juice mixture to the well and stir just until moist. Fold in the cranberries and almonds. Pour batter into the prepared pan.

Bake 50–55 minutes or until a wooden pick inserted in the center comes out clean. Transfer cake to a cooling rack and cool in pan 10 minutes. Remove cake from pan and cool completely on rack. **Makes 18 servings.**

NUTRITION PER SERVING (1 SLICE):
CALORIES 283; FAT 8.6G (SAT 0.8G, MONO 4.9G, POLY 2.4G);
PROTEIN 4.5G; CHOLESTEROL 23.3MG; CARBOHYDRATE 47.8G.

Sour Cream Streusel Coffee Cake

Coffee cakes are among the most popular of comfort foods, welcome at breakfast, lunch, afternoon tea, dinner, and the eponymous coffee breaks. Many versions of cinnamon coffee cake exist, but this streusel-filled sour cream one is an especial favorite. Good luck convincing the lucky tasters that it's significantly lower in fat and calories than the fully loaded variety.

NONSTICK BAKING SPRAY WITH FLOUR	2 LARGE EGG WHITES
¼ CUP PACKED DARK BROWN SUGAR	1 LARGE EGG
¼ CUP COARSELY CHOPPED PECANS	1 CUP FAT-FREE SOUR CREAM
1 TEASPOON GROUND CINNAMON	1 TEASPOON VANILLA EXTRACT
2 CUPS SUGAR	1 CUP ALL-PURPOSE FLOUR
10 TABLESPOONS (1 ¼ STICKS) BUTTER, ROOM TEMPERATURE	1 CUP WHOLE WHEAT PASTRY FLOUR (OR ALL-PURPOSE FLOUR)
4 OUNCES (½ OF AN 8-OUNCE PACKAGE) FAT-FREE CREAM CHEESE, ROOM TEMPERATURE	½ TEASPOON BAKING POWDER
	½ TEASPOON BAKING SODA
	¼ TEASPOON SALT

Preheat oven to 350°F. Spray a 12-cup Bundt pan with nonstick baking spray with flour.

In a small bowl combine the brown sugar, pecans, and cinnamon to make the streusel filling.

In a large bowl beat the sugar, butter, and cream cheese with an electric mixer at medium speed until well blended (about 5 minutes). Add the egg whites and egg, one at a time, beating well after each addition.

In a small bowl whisk the sour cream and vanilla until blended. In a medium bowl whisk the flours, baking powder, baking soda, and salt. Add the flour mixture to butter mixture alternately with the sour cream mixture, beginning and ending with the flour mixture.

Spoon half the batter into bottom of the prepared pan. Sprinkle evenly with the streusel. Spoon the remaining batter over streusel, spreading evenly to cover.

Bake 1 hour or until a wooden pick inserted in the center comes out clean. Transfer cake to a cooling rack and cool in pan 10 minutes. Remove cake from pan and cool completely on rack. **Makes 16 servings.**

NUTRITION PER SERVING (1 SLICE):
CALORIES 270; FAT 9.4G (SAT 4.1G, MONO 3.9G, POLY 0.8G);
PROTEIN 4.1G; CHOLESTEROL 35.4MG; CARBOHYDRATE 43.3G.

Polenta Pound Cake

Cornmeal gives this cake a coarse texture that is a delightful foil for the buttery batter and zing of citrus zests. Fresh berries or sweet summer apricots are terrific accompaniments.

NONSTICK BAKING SPRAY WITH FLOUR	5 LARGE EGGS, SEPARATED
⅔ CUP BUTTER, ROOM TEMPERATURE	1 CUP FAT-FREE SOUR CREAM
2 TEASPOONS GRATED LEMON ZEST	1 CUP YELLOW CORNMEAL
2 TEASPOONS GRATED ORANGE ZEST	2 CUPS ALL-PURPOSE FLOUR
1½ TEASPOONS VANILLA EXTRACT	½ TEASPOON SALT
2 CUPS SUGAR, DIVIDED USE	½ TEASPOON BAKING SODA

Preheat oven to 325°F. Spray a 12-cup Bundt pan with nonstick baking spray with flour.

In a large bowl beat the butter, lemon zest, orange zest, vanilla, and 1¾ cups of the sugar with an electric mixer at medium speed until light and fluffy (about 5 minutes). Add the egg yolks, one at a time, beating well after each addition. Beat in the sour cream until blended.

In a medium bowl whisk the cornmeal, flour, salt, and baking soda. Add the flour mixture to the butter mixture, stirring until just combined.

In a large bowl beat the egg whites with an electric mixer at high speed until foamy. Gradually add remaining ¼ cup sugar, 1 tablespoon at a time, beating until stiff peaks form. Gently stir one-fourth of the egg white mixture into the batter, then gently fold in the remaining egg white mixture. Pour batter into the prepared pan.

Bake 45–50 minutes or until a wooden pick inserted in the center comes out clean. Transfer cake to a cooling rack and cool in pan 15 minutes. Remove cake from pan and cool completely on rack. **Makes 18 servings.**

NUTRITION PER SERVING (1 SLICE):
CALORIES 256; FAT 9.0G (SAT 4.1G, MONO 3.6G, POLY 0.6G);
PROTEIN 4.3G; CHOLESTEROL 79.3MG; CARBOHYDRATE 40.4G.

Tart Cherry–Almond Pound Cake

Tart, dried cherries take center stage in this version of an old favorite.

NONSTICK BAKING SPRAY WITH FLOUR

½ CUP TART DRIED CHERRIES, FINELY CHOPPED

½ CUP AMARETTO (ALMOND-FLAVORED LIQUEUR)

1¼ CUPS SUGAR

1 CUP PACKED LIGHT BROWN SUGAR

¾ CUP (1½ STICKS) UNSALTED BUTTER, ROOM TEMPERATURE

2 TEASPOONS VANILLA EXTRACT

3 LARGE EGGS

1½ CUPS ALL-PURPOSE FLOUR

1½ CUPS WHOLE WHEAT PASTRY FLOUR (OR ALL-PURPOSE FLOUR)

1 TEASPOON BAKING POWDER

½ TEASPOON SALT

½ TEASPOON GROUND MACE

1 CUP FAT-FREE MILK

2 TABLESPOONS POWDERED SUGAR

Place the cherries in a small bowl. Bring the Amaretto to a boil in a small saucepan over medium-high heat; pour over the cherries. Cover and let stand 30 minutes.

Preheat oven to 350°F. Spray a 12-cup Bundt pan with nonstick baking spray with flour.

In a large bowl beat the sugar, brown sugar, butter, and vanilla with an electric mixer at medium speed until well blended (about 5 minutes). Add eggs, one at a time, beating well after each addition.

In a medium bowl whisk the flours, baking powder, salt, and mace. Add the flour mixture to the butter mixture alternately with the milk, beginning and ending with the flour mixture. Stir in the cherry mixture until blended. Pour batter into the prepared pan.

Bake 50–55 minutes or until a wooden pick inserted in the center comes out clean. Transfer cake to a cooling rack and cool in pan 20 minutes. Remove cake from pan and cool completely on rack. Sprinkle with powdered sugar. **Makes 18 servings.**

NUTRITION PER SERVING (1 SLICE):
CALORIES 293; FAT 9.2G (SAT 4.4G, MONO 3.7G, POLY 0.5G);
PROTEIN 3.7G; CHOLESTEROL 57.1MG; CARBOHYDRATE 47G.

Orange Pound Cake

While this sophisticated pound cake is delicious on its own, you can further enhance it with fresh orange segments.

NONSTICK BAKING SPRAY WITH FLOUR

2 CUPS SUGAR

¾ CUP (1½ STICKS) UNSALTED BUTTER, ROOM TEMPERATURE

1½ TABLESPOONS GRATED ORANGE ZEST

3 LARGE EGGS

¾ CUP FAT-FREE BUTTERMILK

1½ TEASPOONS VANILLA EXTRACT

5 TABLESPOONS FRESH ORANGE JUICE, DIVIDED USE

4 TABLESPOONS GRAND MARNIER (OR OTHER ORANGE-FLAVORED LIQUEUR), DIVIDED USE

2½ CUPS ALL-PURPOSE FLOUR

½ TEASPOON BAKING POWDER

½ TEASPOON BAKING SODA

¼ TEASPOON SALT

¾ CUP POWDERED SUGAR

1 TABLESPOON UNSALTED BUTTER, MELTED

Preheat oven to 350°F. Spray a 12-cup Bundt pan with nonstick baking spray with flour.

In a large bowl beat the sugar, butter, and orange zest with an electric mixer at medium speed until well blended (about 5 minutes). Add eggs, one at a time, beating well after each addition.

In a small bowl whisk the buttermilk, vanilla, 4 tablespoons orange juice, and 2½ tablespoons liqueur until blended. In a medium bowl whisk the flour, baking powder, baking soda, and salt. Add the flour mixture to the butter mixture alternately with the buttermilk mixture, beginning and ending with the flour mixture. Pour batter into the prepared pan.

Bake 1 hour and 35 minutes or until a wooden pick inserted in the center comes out clean. Transfer cake to a cooling rack and cool in pan 10 minutes. Remove cake from pan and cool completely on rack.

In a small bowl whisk the powdered sugar, melted butter, remaining 1 tablespoon orange juice, and remaining 2 tablespoons liqueur until smooth. Brush or drizzle over warm cake. Cool completely. **Makes 18 servings.**

NUTRITION PER SERVING (1 SLICE):
CALORIES 270; FAT 9.8G (SAT 4.7G, MONO 4.0G, POLY 0.5G);
PROTEIN 3.3G; CHOLESTEROL 58.8MG; CARBOHYDRATE 41.7G.

Rum Raisin Pound Cake

Raisins and dark rum mingle with brown sugar and butter in this lighter version of an all-American pound cake. It's a showstopper.

NONSTICK BAKING SPRAY WITH FLOUR	1 CUP SEEDLESS RAISINS
2 CUPS PACKED DARK BROWN SUGAR	2 CUPS ALL-PURPOSE FLOUR
⅔ CUP UNSALTED BUTTER, ROOM TEMPERATURE	1 CUP WHOLE WHEAT PASTRY FLOUR (OR ALL-PURPOSE FLOUR)
2 LARGE EGGS	2 TEASPOONS BAKING POWDER
1 LARGE EGG WHITE	1 TEASPOON BAKING SODA
1 CUP LOW-FAT BUTTERMILK	½ TEASPOON GROUND NUTMEG
½ CUP DARK RUM	¼ TEASPOON SALT
2 TEASPOONS VANILLA EXTRACT	

Preheat oven to 350°F. Spray a 12-cup Bundt pan with nonstick baking spray with flour.

In a large bowl beat the brown sugar and butter with an electric mixer at medium speed until well blended (about 5 minutes). Add eggs and egg white, one at a time, beating well after each addition.

In a small bowl whisk the buttermilk, rum, and vanilla until blended.

In another small bowl toss the raisins with 1 tablespoon of the all-purpose flour. In a medium bowl whisk the remaining all-purpose flour, whole wheat pastry flour, baking powder, baking soda, nutmeg, and salt. Add flour mixture to butter mixture alternately with buttermilk mixture, beginning and ending with flour mixture. Fold in raisin mixture. Pour batter into prepared pan.

Bake 45–50 minutes or until a wooden pick inserted in the center comes out clean. Transfer cake to a cooling rack and cool in pan 10 minutes. Remove cake from pan and cool completely on rack. **Makes 18 servings.**

NUTRITION PER SERVING (1 SLICE):
CALORIES 281; FAT 8.3G (SAT 4.0G, MONO 3.3G, POLY 0.4G);
PROTEIN 3.9G; CHOLESTEROL 43.8MG; CARBOHYDRATE 45.3G.

Pumpkin Pound Cake

This pretty pound cake is an impressive alternative to classic pumpkin pie. Moist, spicy, and drizzled with a tangy buttermilk icing, it adds up to one irresistible autumn treat.

NONSTICK BAKING SPRAY WITH FLOUR

1¼ CUPS SUGAR

½ CUP (1 STICK) UNSALTED BUTTER, ROOM TEMPERATURE

2 LARGE EGGS

2 LARGE EGG WHITES

1⅓ CUPS CANNED SOLID-PACK PUMPKIN (FROM A 15-OUNCE CAN)

1 CUP PLUS 3 TABLESPOONS LOW-FAT BUTTERMILK, DIVIDED USE

2 TEASPOONS VANILLA EXTRACT

1¼ CUPS ALL-PURPOSE FLOUR

1 CUP WHOLE WHEAT PASTRY FLOUR (OR ALL-PURPOSE FLOUR)

2 TEASPOONS BAKING POWDER

1 TEASPOON BAKING SODA

1 TABLESPOON GROUND GINGER

2 TEASPOONS CINNAMON

1 TEASPOON GROUND ALLSPICE

½ TEASPOON SALT

1½ CUPS POWDERED SUGAR

Preheat oven to 350°F. Spray a 12-cup Bundt pan with nonstick baking spray with flour.

In a large bowl beat the sugar and butter with an electric mixer at medium speed until well blended (about 5 minutes). Add eggs and egg whites, one at a time, beating well after each addition.

In a small bowl whisk the pumpkin, 1 cup buttermilk, and vanilla until blended. In a medium bowl whisk the flours, baking powder, baking soda, ginger, cinnamon, allspice, and salt. Add the flour mixture to the butter mixture alternately with the pumpkin mixture, beginning and ending with the flour mixture. Pour batter into the prepared pan.

Bake 45–50 minutes or until a wooden pick inserted in the center comes out clean. Transfer cake to a cooling rack and cool in pan 10 minutes.

While cake is cooling, whisk together powdered sugar and remaining 3 tablespoons buttermilk. Remove cake from pan, transfer to rack, and brush or drizzle icing over warm cake. Cool cake completely. **Makes 16 servings.**

NUTRITION PER SERVING (1 SLICE):
CALORIES 243; FAT 7.3G (SAT 3.5G, MONO 2.9G, POLY 0.4G);
PROTEIN 4.0G; CHOLESTEROL 44MG; CARBOHYDRATE 41.2G.

Charlotte's Sherry Pound Cake

Christmas in my childhood home was a series of strategic baking procedures. My mother had a plan, everyone had a job, and by some minor miracle, we would somehow deploy enough cookies and cakes to feed a small army. Time was premium. To compensate, my mom had a collection of simple recipes to counter her more labor-intensive ones to preserve everyone's (especially her) sanity. This is an enlightened version of a cake she still makes often, and always receives requests for the recipe. It's good, easy, and practical; everyone loves the sherry and nutmeg, even though they rarely guess that they're in the cake.

NONSTICK BAKING SPRAY WITH FLOUR	2 TEASPOONS VANILLA EXTRACT
¾ CUP (1½ STICKS) BUTTER, ROOM TEMPERATURE	2 CUPS ALL-PURPOSE FLOUR
1¼ CUPS SUGAR	1¼ CUPS WHOLE WHEAT PASTRY FLOUR (OR ALL-PURPOSE FLOUR)
1¼ CUPS PACKED LIGHT BROWN SUGAR	1 TEASPOON GROUND NUTMEG
2 LARGE EGGS	½ TEASPOON BAKING SODA
2 LARGE EGG WHITES	¼ TEASPOON SALT
¾ CUP REDUCED-FAT SOUR CREAM	2 TABLESPOONS POWDERED SUGAR
½ CUP SWEET SHERRY	

Preheat oven to 325°F. Spray a 12-cup Bundt pan with nonstick baking spray with flour.

In a large bowl beat the butter, sugar, and brown sugar with an electric mixer at medium speed until well blended (about 5 minutes). Add eggs and egg whites, one at a time, beating well after each addition.

In a small bowl whisk the sour cream, Sherry, and vanilla until blended. In a medium bowl whisk the flours, nutmeg, baking soda, and salt. Add the flour mixture to butter mixture alternately with the sour cream mixture, beginning and ending with the flour mixture. Pour batter into the prepared pan.

Bake 1 hour and 10 minutes or until a wooden pick inserted in the center comes out clean. Transfer cake to a cooling rack and cool in pan 10 minutes. Remove cake from pan and cool completely on rack. Sprinkle cake with powdered sugar. **Makes 18 servings.**

NUTRITION PER SERVING (1 SLICE):
CALORIES 292; FAT 9.7G (SAT 4.8G, MONO 3.8G, POLY 0.5G);
PROTEIN 3.6G; CHOLESTEROL 46.9MG; CARBOHYDRATE 44.4G.

Carrot Cake Bundt

Carrot cakes have been a part of American baking for years, and they remain a favorite dessert, whether in the South, Midwest or along the coasts. This version skips the layers in favor of the ease of a Bundt pan. The rich cream cheese frosting everyone expects (and loves) is likewise transformed into a pourable, lemon-accented icing that's as delicious as it is beautiful.

NONSTICK BAKING SPRAY WITH FLOUR

1¼ CUPS ALL-PURPOSE FLOUR

1¼ CUPS WHOLE WHEAT PASTRY FLOUR (OR ALL-PURPOSE FLOUR)

2 TEASPOONS BAKING SODA

2 TEASPOONS GROUND GINGER

1½ TEASPOONS GROUND CINNAMON

½ TEASPOON BAKING POWDER

½ TEASPOON SALT

½ TEASPOON GROUND NUTMEG

2 CUPS COARSELY SHREDDED PEELED CARROTS

1½ CUPS PACKED LIGHT BROWN SUGAR

1 CUP GOLDEN RAISINS

1 CUP FAT-FREE MILK

6 TABLESPOONS BUTTER, MELTED

2 LARGE EGGS, LIGHTLY BEATEN

1 RECIPE LEMON CREAM CHEESE ICING (SEE PAGE 143)

Preheat oven to 350°F. Spray a 12-cup Bundt pan with nonstick baking spray with flour.

In a large bowl whisk the flours, baking soda, ginger, cinnamon, baking powder, salt, and nutmeg until blended. In a medium bowl combine the carrots, brown sugar, golden raisins, milk, melted butter, and eggs until well blended.

Add the carrot mixture to the flour mixture, stirring just until the flour mixture is moistened. Pour batter into the prepared pan.

Bake 1 hour and 5 minutes or until a wooden pick inserted in the center comes out clean. Transfer cake to a cooling rack and cool in pan 10 minutes. Remove cake from pan and cool completely on rack.

Prepare Lemon Cream Cheese Icing. Drizzle lemon icing over top of cake, allowing icing to flow down sides. **Makes 18 servings.**

NUTRITION PER SERVING (1 SLICE):
CALORIES 243; FAT 5.9G (SAT 2.9G, MONO 2.2G, POLY 0.3G);
PROTEIN 3.9G; CHOLESTEROL 38.1MG; CARBOHYDRATE 44.7G.

3. LAYER

Cakes

CHOCOLATE BIRTHDAY **CAKE** WITH CHOCOLATE CREAM CHEESE FROSTING, ANGELIC RASPBERRIES AND CREAM **CAKE**, TIRAMISÙ TORTE, ITALIAN MERINGUE LAYER **CAKE**, TENNESSEE JAM **CAKE** WITH BROWN SUGAR FUDGE FROSTING, OLD-FASHIONED YELLOW LAYER **CAKE** WITH CHOCOLATE SILK FROSTING, TRIPLE-LAYER COCONUT **CAKE**, LEMON CURD LAYER **CAKE**, BLACKBERRY LAYER **CAKE**, APPLESAUCE **CAKE** WITH CARAMEL FROSTING, DULCE DE LECHE LAYER **CAKE**, CHOCOLATE-LAVENDER LAYER **CAKE**, FRESH LIME LAYER **CAKE**, SPICED LAYER **CAKE** WITH CREAM CHEESE FROSTING, MOCHA BUTTERCREAM **CAKE**, ITALIAN CREAM **CAKE** . . .

Chocolate Birthday Cake

WITH CHOCOLATE CREAM CHEESE FROSTING

Here's a classic chocolate layer cake with a new-fashioned nutrition profile. The chocolate–cream cheese frosting provides a subtle and slightly tangy contrast to the dark chocolate cake.

NONSTICK BAKING SPRAY WITH FLOUR

1⅓ CUPS SUGAR

⅓ CUP TRANS-FAT-FREE VEGETABLE SHORT-
ENING (E.G., CRISCO® ZERO TRANS FAT
SHORTENING)

2 TEASPOONS VANILLA EXTRACT

3 LARGE EGGS

1¾ CUPS ALL-PURPOSE FLOUR

½ CUP UNSWEETENED COCOA POWDER (NOT
DUTCH PROCESS)

1 TEASPOON BAKING POWDER

1 TEASPOON BAKING SODA

½ TEASPOON SALT

1¼ CUPS FAT-FREE MILK

1 RECIPE CHOCOLATE-CREAM CHEESE
FROSTING (SEE PAGE 149)

Preheat oven to 350°F. Spray two 8-inch round cake pans with nonstick baking spray with flour.

In a large bowl beat the sugar, shortening and vanilla with an electric mixer at medium speed until well blended (about 5 minutes). Add the eggs, one at a time, beating well after each addition.

In a medium bowl whisk the flour, cocoa powder, baking powder, baking soda and salt. Add the flour mixture to the sugar mixture alternately with milk, beginning and ending with flour mixture, beating well after each addition. Spoon batter into prepared pans. Sharply tap pans once on the counter to remove air bubbles.

Bake 28–30 minutes or until cakes spring back when touched lightly in the center. Cool in pans 5 minutes on wire racks. Remove cakes from pans and cool completely on wire racks.

Prepare Chocolate Cream Cheese Frosting. Place one cake layer on a serving plate and spread with ½ cup frosting. Top with remaining cake layer and spread remaining frosting on sides and top of cake. Cover and chill at least 1 hour. **Makes 18 servings.**

NUTRITION PER SERVING (1 SLICE):
CALORIES 280; FAT 9.2G (SAT 3.1G, MONO 4.1G, POLY 1.5G);
PROTEIN 5.1G; CHOLESTEROL 45.9MG; CARBOHYDRATE 47.9G.

Angelic Raspberries and Cream Cake

Here, lush summer raspberries are framed by fluffy angel food cake and a creamy filling and frosting that underlines their tart juiciness.

1 RECIPE CLASSIC ANGEL FOOD CAKE (SEE PAGE 20)	3 TABLESPOONS ORANGE-FLAVORED LIQUEUR, DIVIDED USE
4 CUPS FRESH RASPBERRIES, DIVIDED USE	1 8-OUNCE CONTAINER FAT-FREE FROZEN WHIPPED TOPPING, THAWED
7 TABLESPOONS SUGAR, DIVIDED USE	OPTIONAL: SMALL MINT LEAVES
1 8-OUNCE PACKAGE ⅓-LESS-FAT CREAM CHEESE, ROOM TEMPERATURE	
6 TABLESPOONS REDUCED-FAT SOUR CREAM, DIVIDED USE	

Prepare Classic Angel Food Cake as directed. Cool completely.

In a medium bowl combine 3½ cups raspberries and 3 tablespoons sugar. Cover and let stand 1 hour. Reserve the other ½ cup berries for garnish.

In a medium bowl beat the cream cheese, 2 tablespoons of the sour cream, and the remaining 4 tablespoons sugar with an electric mixer at medium speed until smooth.

Cut the cake horizontally into 3 layers using a serrated knife. Place bottom layer, cut side up, on a serving plate. Brush with 1 tablespoon liqueur, then spread half of cream cheese mixture over cake. Spoon half of the raspberries over the cream cheese mixture using a slotted spoon. Repeat layers, ending with cake and liqueur.

In a medium bowl combine the whipped topping and remaining 4 tablespoons sour cream until blended. Spread whipped topping mixture over top and sides of cake. Chill 30 minutes. Arrange remaining raspberries and (optional) mint leaves on top of cake before serving. **Makes 16 servings.**

NUTRITION PER SERVING (1 SLICE):
CALORIES 240; FAT 3.9G (SAT 2.4G, MONO 1.1G, POLY 0.3G);
PROTEIN 5.8G; CHOLESTEROL 12.2MG; CARBOHYDRATE 44.9G.

Tiramisù Torte

Loosely translated, tiramisù means "pick-me-up" in Italian—and this layer-cake rendition certainly does just that. Making the angel food cake a day ahead makes this especially easy.

1   RECIPE CLASSIC ANGEL FOOD CAKE (SEE PAGE 20)

1   8-OUNCE PACKAGE ⅓-LESS-FAT CREAM CHEESE, ROOM TEMPERATURE

¼   CUP POWDERED SUGAR

3   TABLESPOONS UNSWEETENED COCOA POWDER (NOT DUTCH PROCESS)

1   TABLESPOON INSTANT ESPRESSO POWDER

2   8-OUNCE CONTAINERS FAT-FREE FROZEN WHIPPED TOPPING, THAWED, DIVIDED USE

5   TABLESPOONS COFFEE-FLAVORED LIQUEUR (E.G., KAHLUA), DIVIDED USE

2   OUNCES BITTERSWEET CHOCOLATE, COARSELY GRATED, DIVIDED USE

1   CUP SLICED ALMONDS, TOASTED

Prepare Classic Angel Food Cake as directed. Cool completely.

In a large bowl beat the cream cheese with an electric mixer at medium speed until smooth. Add the powdered sugar, cocoa powder, espresso powder, 1 cup of the whipped topping and 2 tablespoons liqueur. Beat until fluffy and smooth. Fold in the remaining whipped topping. Set frosting aside.

Cut the cake horizontally into 3 layers using a serrated knife. Place bottom layer, cut side up, on a serving plate. Brush with 1 tablespoon liqueur, then spread with 1 cup frosting. Sprinkle with one-third of the grated chocolate. Repeat layering with cake, liqueur, frosting, and grated chocolate, ending with cake and liqueur.

Spread remaining frosting over top and sides of cake. Press almonds onto sides of cake. Sprinkle top with remaining chocolate. Chill until ready to serve. **Makes 16 servings.**

NUTRITION PER SERVING (1 SLICE):
CALORIES 251; FAT 7.0G (SAT 2.2G, MONO 3.4G, POLY 1.2G);
PROTEIN 7.9G; CHOLESTEROL 1.1MG; CARBOHYDRATE 38.5G.

Italian Meringue Layer Cake

As much as I love a good chocolate layer cake, this elegant alternative—a light, delicious layering of buttery cake and meringue frosting—tops my list of favorites for special occasion splurges. It's not the best cake to choose in warm weather, though, so save it for spring soirees or your next New Year's Eve celebration.

NONSTICK BAKING SPRAY WITH FLOUR

2 CUPS SUGAR

¾ CUP (1½ STICKS) UNSALTED BUTTER, ROOM TEMPERATURE

3 LARGE EGGS

1 TEASPOON VANILLA EXTRACT

½ TEASPOON ALMOND EXTRACT

3 CUPS CAKE FLOUR

½ TEASPOON BAKING POWDER

½ TEASPOON BAKING SODA

½ TEASPOON SALT

¾ CUP FAT-FREE BUTTERMILK

1 RECIPE ITALIAN MERINGUE FROSTING (SEE PAGE 161)

Preheat oven to 350°F. Spray two 8-inch round cake pans with nonstick baking spray with flour.

In a large bowl beat the sugar and butter with an electric mixer at medium speed for 5 minutes. Add eggs, one at a time, beating well after each addition. Beat in vanilla and almond extract.

In a medium bowl whisk the flour, baking powder, baking soda, and salt. Add the flour mixture and buttermilk alternately to the sugar mixture, beginning and ending with the flour mixture, mixing well after each addition. Pour batter into the prepared cake pans. Sharply tap pans once on counter to remove air bubbles.

Bake 28–30 minutes or until a wooden pick inserted in the center comes out clean. Cool cake in pans for 10 minutes on a wire rack. Remove cakes from pans and cool completely on wire rack.

Prepare the Italian Meringue Frosting. Place one of the cake layers on a serving plate. Spread with ½ cup frosting. Top with remaining cake layer. Spread remaining frosting over top and sides of cake. **Makes 18 servings.**

NUTRITION PER SERVING (1 SLICE):
CALORIES 282; FAT 9.1G (SAT 4.3G, MONO 3.6G, POLY 0.5G);
PROTEIN 3.4G; CHOLESTEROL 56.4MG; CARBOHYDRATE 47.7G.

Tennessee Jam Cake

WITH BROWN SUGAR FUDGE FROSTING

Spice cake never tasted so good. This now-classic cake is the invention of an innovative southern baker from years past, and oh, what a combination of flavors: blackberry jam, buttery-brown sugar layers, and a brown sugar fudge frosting make it nothing short of magnificent.

NONSTICK BAKING SPRAY WITH FLOUR

¾ CUP PACKED DARK BROWN SUGAR

½ CUP SUGAR

½ CUP (1 STICK) BUTTER, ROOM TEMPERATURE

2 LARGE EGGS

1 LARGE EGG WHITE

2 TEASPOONS VANILLA EXTRACT

1 CUP ALL-PURPOSE FLOUR

1 CUP WHOLE WHEAT PASTRY FLOUR (OR ALL-PURPOSE FLOUR)

1 TEASPOON GROUND CINNAMON

½ TEASPOON GROUND NUTMEG

½ TEASPOON BAKING SODA

½ TEASPOON SALT

¼ TEASPOON GROUND CLOVES

1 CUP LOW-FAT BUTTERMILK

⅓ CUP SEEDLESS BLACKBERRY JAM

1 RECIPE BROWN SUGAR FUDGE FROSTING (SEE PAGE 157)

OPTIONAL: 2 TABLESPOONS CHOPPED TOASTED PECANS

Preheat oven to 350°F. Spray two 8-inch round cake pans with nonstick baking spray with flour.

In a large bowl beat the brown sugar, sugar, and butter with an electric mixer at medium speed until well blended (about 5 minutes). Add the eggs and egg white, one at a time, beating well after each addition. Beat in the vanilla.

Whisk the flours, cinnamon, nutmeg, baking soda, salt, and cloves in a medium bowl. Add the flour mixture to the sugar mixture alternately with buttermilk, beginning and ending with the flour mixture, beating well after each addition. Pour batter into the prepared pans. Sharply tap pans once on counter to remove air bubbles.

Bake 22–25 minutes or until a wooden pick inserted in the center comes out clean. Cool in pans 10 minutes on a wire rack. Remove cakes from pans and cool completely on wire rack.

Prepare the Brown Sugar Fudge Frosting. Place 1 cake layer on a plate and spoon blackberry jam onto the cake layer, spreading to cover. Top with remaining cake layer. Spread the frosting over top and sides of cake. If desired, sprinkle top of cake with the pecans. Store cake loosely covered in refrigerator. **Makes 18 servings.**

NUTRITION PER SERVING (1 SLICE):
CALORIES 296; FAT 8.1G (SAT 3.9G, MONO 3.2G, POLY 0.4G);
PROTEIN 3.1G; CHOLESTEROL 43.4MG; CARBOHYDRATE 52.8G.

Old-Fashioned Yellow Layer Cake

WITH CHOCOLATE SILK FROSTING

This luscious cake takes its cues from quintessential birthday cake, combining tender vanilla cake layers and a lusciously chocolate frosting.

NONSTICK BAKING SPRAY WITH FLOUR

1⅔ CUPS SUGAR

½ CUP (1 STICK) BUTTER, ROOM TEMPERATURE

1 TABLESPOON VANILLA EXTRACT

3 LARGE EGGS

2¼ CUPS ALL-PURPOSE FLOUR

2¼ TEASPOONS BAKING POWDER

½ TEASPOON SALT

1¼ CUPS FAT-FREE MILK

1 RECIPE CHOCOLATE SILK FROSTING (SEE PAGE 152)

Preheat oven to 350°F. Spray two 9-inch round cake pans with nonstick baking spray with flour.

In a large bowl beat the sugar, butter, and vanilla with an electric mixer at medium speed until well blended (about 5 minutes). Add eggs, one at a time, beating well after each addition.

In a medium bowl whisk the flour, baking powder, and salt. Add the flour mixture to the sugar mixture alternately with milk, beginning and ending with the flour mixture. Pour batter into prepared pans. Sharply tap pans once on counter to remove air bubbles.

Bake 27–30 minutes or until a wooden pick inserted in the center comes out clean. Cool in pans 10 minutes on a wire rack. Remove cakes from pans and cool completely on wire rack.

Prepare the Chocolate Silk Frosting. Place 1 cake layer on a plate and spread with ½ cup frosting. Top with remaining layer. Spread remaining frosting over top and sides of cake. Store cake loosely covered in refrigerator. **Makes 18 servings.**

NUTRITION PER SERVING (1 SLICE):
CALORIES 247; FAT 9.4G (SAT 4.7G, MONO 3.5G, POLY 0.5G);
PROTEIN 4.9G; CHOLESTEROL 50MG; CARBOHYDRATE 37.6G.

Triple-Layer Coconut Cake

Although this cake calls for coconut milk in the batter and a toasted flaked coconut finish, don't be tempted to omit the coconut extract—it really adds depth to the overall coconut flavor.

NONSTICK BAKING SPRAY WITH FLOUR

2 CUPS SUGAR

6 TABLESPOONS (¾ STICK) BUTTER, ROOM TEMPERATURE

1 TEASPOON COCONUT EXTRACT

2 LARGE EGGS

2 LARGE EGG WHITES

2½ CUPS CAKE FLOUR

2 TEASPOONS BAKING POWDER

½ TEASPOON SALT

¾ CUP CANNED LIGHT COCONUT MILK

1 RECIPE FLUFFY COCONUT BUTTERCREAM (SEE PAGE 160)

¼ CUP TOASTED FLAKED SWEETENED COCONUT

Preheat oven to 350°F. Spray three 8-inch round cake pans with nonstick baking spray with flour.

In a medium bowl beat the sugar, butter, and coconut extract with an electric mixer at medium speed for 2 minutes or until well blended. Add eggs and egg whites to the sugar mixture; beat well.

In a medium bowl whisk the flour, baking powder, and salt. Add the flour mixture and coconut milk alternately to the sugar mixture, beginning and ending with the flour mixture. Spoon batter into prepared pans. Sharply tap the pans once on countertop to remove air bubbles.

Bake 22–25 minutes or until a wooden pick inserted in the center comes out clean. Cool in pans 10 minutes on wire racks. Remove cakes from pans and cool completely on wire racks.

Prepare the Fluffy Coconut Buttercream. Place 1 cake layer on a plate and spread with 1 cup frosting. Repeat twice with cake layers and 1 cup frosting, ending with a cake layer; spread remaining frosting over top and sides of cake. Sprinkle with toasted coconut. Chill until set. **Makes 18 servings.**

NUTRITION PER SERVING (1 SLICE):
CALORIES 267; FAT 8.3G (SAT 4.4G, MONO 3.1G, POLY 0.4G);
PROTEIN 3.3G; CHOLESTEROL 41.4MG; CARBOHYDRATE 45.8G.

Lemon Curd Layer Cake

Plain yogurt and vegetable oil moisten the cake layers, and lemon curd intensifies the citrus flavor. If time is short, ready-made lemon curd (located where the jams are shelved in the supermarket) works just fine. The gorgeous, snow-white frosting makes this a showstopper in looks, as well as taste.

1   RECIPE LEMON CURD (SEE PAGE 166)
    NONSTICK BAKING SPRAY WITH FLOUR
1¾ CUPS SUGAR
¼   CUP (½ STICK) BUTTER, ROOM
    TEMPERATURE
1½ TABLESPOONS CANOLA OIL
2½ TEASPOONS VANILLA EXTRACT
2   LARGE EGG WHITES

3⅓ CUPS CAKE FLOUR
2   TEASPOONS BAKING POWDER
¾   TEASPOON SALT
½   TEASPOON BAKING SODA
1⅔ CUPS FAT-FREE MILK
½   CUP PLAIN FAT-FREE YOGURT
1   RECIPE FLUFFY BUTTERCREAM (SEE PAGE
    160)

Prepare Lemon Curd as directed.

Preheat oven to 350°F. Spray three 8-inch round cake pans with nonstick baking spray with flour.

In a large bowl beat the sugar, butter, canola oil, and vanilla with an electric mixer at medium speed until well blended (about 5 minutes). Add egg whites, one at a time, beating well after each addition.

In a medium bowl whisk the flour, baking powder, salt, and baking soda. In a small bowl whisk the milk and yogurt. Add the flour mixture to the butter mixture alternately with milk mixture, beginning and ending with the flour mixture. Pour cake batter into the prepared pans. Sharply tap pans once on counter to remove air bubbles.

Bake 23–26 minutes or until a wooden pick inserted in the center comes out clean. Cool in pans 10 minutes on wire racks. Remove cakes from pans and cool completely on wire racks.

Prepare the Fluffy Buttercream. Place 1 cake layer on a plate and spread with half of the lemon curd. Top with another cake layer and spread with remaining lemon curd. Top with last cake layer and spread frosting over top and sides of cake. **Makes 18 servings.**

NUTRITION PER SERVING (1 SLICE):
CALORIES 295; FAT 7.3G (SAT 3.1G, MONO 3.1G, POLY 0.7G);
PROTEIN 4.3G; CHOLESTEROL 36.7MG; CARBOHYDRATE 54G.

Blackberry Layer Cake

A cool, fluffy frosting, jam filling, and citrus-scented cake layers make this a perfect peak-of-summer cake. The fresh blackberries add a lush, fruity finish and tame the sweetness of the cake with their slightly tart flavor.

NONSTICK BAKING SPRAY WITH FLOUR	1 CUP FAT-FREE MILK
9 TABLESPOONS BUTTER, ROOM TEMPERATURE	1 CUP REDUCED-FAT SOUR CREAM, DIVIDED USE
2 CUPS SUGAR, DIVIDED USE	½ CUP FRESH ORANGE JUICE
1 TABLESPOON GRATED ORANGE ZEST	½ CUP SEEDLESS BLACKBERRY JAM, MELTED
1 TABLESPOON VANILLA EXTRACT	AND COOLED
4 LARGE EGG WHITES	2 CUPS FROZEN FAT-FREE WHIPPED
3 CUPS CAKE FLOUR	TOPPING, THAWED
1½ TEASPOONS BAKING SODA	2 CUPS FRESH BLACKBERRIES
¾ TEASPOON SALT	OPTIONAL: FRESH MINT LEAVES FOR GARNISH

Preheat oven to 350°F. Spray two 9-inch round cake pans with nonstick baking spray with flour.

In a large bowl beat the butter and 1¾ cups of the sugar with an electric mixer at medium speed until light and fluffy (about 5 minutes). Beat in orange zest and vanilla. Add egg whites, one at a time, beating well after each addition.

In a medium bowl whisk the flour, baking soda, and salt. In a small bowl whisk the milk and ¾ cup of the sour cream. Add the flour mixture and the milk mixture alternately to the butter mixture, beginning and ending with the flour mixture. Pour batter into the prepared pans. Sharply tap pans once on counter to remove air bubbles.

Bake 23–26 minutes or until a wooden pick inserted in the center comes out clean. Cool in pans 20 minutes on a wire rack. Remove cakes from pans and cool completely on wire rack.

In a small bowl combine orange juice and remaining ¼ cup sugar, stirring until sugar dissolves. Pierce the cake layers liberally with a wooden pick. Slowly drizzle the orange juice mixture over cake layers.

Place 1 cake layer on a plate and spread with blackberry jam. Top with remaining cake layer. Fold remaining ¼ cup sour cream into whipped topping and spread mixture over top and sides of cake. Arrange blackberries on top of cake and garnish with mint, if desired. Cover and chill at least 2 hours. **Makes 16 servings.**

NUTRITION PER SERVING (1 SLICE):
CALORIES 294; FAT 7.4G (SAT 4.1G, MONO 2.5G, POLY 0.4G);
PROTEIN 3.8G; CHOLESTEROL 17.9MG; CARBOHYDRATE 55.8G.

Applesauce Cake

WITH CARAMEL FROSTING

Whether you use store-bought applesauce or make your own, this humble cake will make it hard to stop after one piece. The caramel frosting clinches it.

	NONSTICK BAKING SPRAY WITH FLOUR	4	TEASPOONS UNSWEETENED COCOA POWDER (NOT DUTCH PROCESS)
1	CUP PACKED DARK BROWN SUGAR	2	TEASPOONS BAKING SODA
1	CUP SUGAR	2	TEASPOONS GROUND CINNAMON
⅓	CUP TRANS-FAT-FREE VEGETABLE SHORT-ENING (E.G., CRISCO® ZERO TRANS FAT SHORTENING)	2	TEASPOONS GROUND NUTMEG
1	TEASPOON VANILLA EXTRACT	½	TEASPOON SALT
2	CUPS UNSWEETENED APPLESAUCE	⅔	CUP RAISINS
3	CUPS ALL-PURPOSE FLOUR	1	RECIPE CARAMEL FROSTING (SEE PAGE 156)

Preheat oven to 350°F. Spray two 9-inch round cake pans with nonstick baking spray with flour.

In a large bowl beat the brown sugar, sugar, shortening, and vanilla with an electric mixer at low speed until well blended (about 5 minutes). Beat in the applesauce until well blended.

In a medium bowl whisk the flour, cocoa powder, baking soda, cinnamon, nutmeg, and salt. Add the flour mixture to the applesauce mixture, beating just until moist. Stir in raisins. Spoon batter into the prepared pans. Sharply tap pans once on counter to remove air bubbles.

Bake 32–35 minutes or until a wooden pick inserted in the center comes out clean. Cool in pans 10 minutes on a wire rack. Remove cakes from pans and cool completely on a wire rack.

Prepare the Caramel Frosting. Place 1 cake layer on a plate. Working quickly, spread with ⅓ cup frosting, then top with remaining cake layer. Spread remaining frosting over top and sides of cake. Store loosely covered in refrigerator. **Makes 18 servings.**

NUTRITION PER SERVING (1 SLICE):
CALORIES 300; FAT 4.8G (SAT 0.6G, MONO 2.6G, POLY 1.3G);
PROTEIN 2.6G; CHOLESTEROL 1.4MG; CARBOHYDRATE 69.1G.

Dulce de Leche Layer Cake

Inspired by Latin America's treasured dessert, this dulce de leche layer cake is an irresistible layering of buttery brown sugar cake and dark golden caramel frosting.

NONSTICK BAKING SPRAY WITH FLOUR

1 CUP PACKED LIGHT BROWN SUGAR

7 TABLESPOONS UNSALTED BUTTER, ROOM TEMPERATURE

2 LARGE EGG WHITES

1 LARGE EGG

2 CUPS CAKE FLOUR

1 TEASPOON BAKING POWDER

½ TEASPOON BAKING SODA

¼ TEASPOON SALT

1 CUP FAT-FREE MILK

1 RECIPE DULCE DE LECHE FROSTING (SEE PAGE 155)

Preheat oven to 350°F. Spray two 8-inch round cake pans with nonstick baking spray with flour.

In a large bowl beat the brown sugar and butter with an electric mixer at medium speed until well blended (about 5 minutes). Add egg whites and egg, beating well.

In a medium bowl whisk the flour, baking powder, baking soda, and salt. Add the flour mixture to the sugar mixture alternately with milk, beginning and ending with the flour mixture. Spoon batter into the prepared pans. Sharply tap pans once on counter to remove air bubbles.

Bake 23–25 minutes or until a wooden pick inserted in the center comes out clean. Cool in pans 10 minutes on a wire rack. Remove cakes from pans and cool completely on wire rack.

Prepare the Dulce de Leche Frosting. Place 1 cake layer on a plate; spread with ⅓ cup frosting. Top with remaining cake layer. Spread remaining frosting over top and sides of cake. **Makes 16 servings.**

NUTRITION PER SERVING (1 SLICE):
CALORIES 278; FAT 8G (SAT 4G, MONO 3.3G, POLY 0.4G);
PROTEIN 3.7G; CHOLESTEROL 34.3MG; CARBOHYDRATE 32.4G.

Chocolate-Lavender Layer Cake

An undoubtedly elegant cake, this confection was inspired by a scoop of chocolate lavender gelato from one of my trips home to the San Francisco Bay Area. Lavender may seem an unusual pairing, but trust me on this one—the sweet, floral notes of the lavender accent the bittersweet qualities of the cocoa powder in perfect harmony.

NONSTICK BAKING SPRAY WITH FLOUR

1⅓ CUPS BOILING WATER, DIVIDED USE

6 TABLESPOONS DRIED LAVENDER

⅔ CUP UNSWEETENED COCOA POWDER (NOT DUTCH PROCESS)

¼ CUP LOW-FAT BUTTERMILK

2 TEASPOONS VANILLA EXTRACT

2 CUPS SUGAR

¼ CUP (½ STICK) UNSALTED BUTTER, ROOM TEMPERATURE

3 LARGE EGG WHITES

1 LARGE EGG

2 CUPS CAKE FLOUR

1 TEASPOON BAKING SODA

¼ TEASPOON SALT

1 RECIPE CHOCOLATE LAVENDER ICING (SEE PAGE 151)

OPTIONAL: FRESH EDIBLE FLOWERS OR CANDIED LILACS FOR GARNISH

Preheat oven to 350°F. Spray two 9-inch round cake pans with nonstick baking spray with flour.

Pour ⅔ cup of the boiling water over lavender and let steep 10 minutes. Strain through a fine sieve into a bowl, discarding lavender. Cool to room temperature.

In a medium bowl whisk the cocoa powder and remaining ⅔ cup boiling water until blended. Cool in freezer 10 minutes. Whisk in the lavender water, buttermilk, and vanilla.

In a large bowl beat the sugar and butter with an electric mixer at medium speed until well blended (about 5 minutes). Add egg whites and egg, one at a time, beating well after each addition.

In a medium bowl whisk the flour, baking soda, and salt. Add the flour mixture and the cocoa mixture alternately to the sugar mixture, beginning and ending with the flour mixture. Pour batter into the prepared cake pans. Sharply tap pans once on counter to remove air bubbles.

Bake 28–30 minutes or until a wooden pick inserted in the center comes out clean. Cool in pans 10 minutes on a wire rack. Remove cakes from pans and cool completely on wire rack.

Prepare the Chocolate Lavender Icing. Place 1 cake layer on a plate and spread with ½ cup icing. Top with another cake layer. Spread remaining icing over top and sides of cake. Garnish with edible flowers or candied lilacs, if desired. Store cake loosely covered in refrigerator. **Makes 16 servings.**

NUTRITION PER SERVING (1 SLICE):
CALORIES 284; FAT 6.6G (SAT 3.7G, MONO 2.3G, POLY 0.3G);
PROTEIN 4.5G; CHOLESTEROL 29.1MG; CARBOHYDRATE 55G.

Fresh Lime Layer Cake

Inspired by key lime pie, this tart, creamy-cool cake uses regular rather than key limes.

1 14-OUNCE CAN FAT-FREE SWEETENED CONDENSED MILK	7 TABLESPOONS CANOLA OIL
6 TABLESPOONS PLUS ⅓ CUP FRESH LIME JUICE (ABOUT 6–7 LIMES), DIVIDED USE	3 TABLESPOONS WATER
3 TEASPOONS FINELY GRATED LIME ZEST, DIVIDED USE	3 EGG YOLKS
2 CUPS CAKE FLOUR	8 EGG WHITES
1¼ CUPS SUGAR, DIVIDED USE	1 TEASPOON CREAM OF TARTAR
2½ TEASPOONS BAKING POWDER	3 TABLESPOONS POWDERED SUGAR
½ TEASPOON SALT	2½ CUPS FAT-FREE FROZEN WHIPPED TOPPING, THAWED
	OPTIONAL: FRESH MINT SPRIGS AND LIME WEDGES

To prepare the filling, stir the sweetened condensed milk, 4 tablespoons of the lime juice, and 1 teaspoon of the lime zest in a small bowl until blended. Cover and chill 3 hours.

Preheat oven to 325°F. Spray the bottoms only (not the sides) of three 8-inch round cake pans with nonstick cooking spray.

In a large bowl whisk the flour, 1 cup of the sugar, baking powder, and ½ teaspoon salt. In a medium bowl whisk the oil, ⅓ cup of the remaining lime juice, 3 tablespoons water, egg yolks, and remaining 2 teaspoons lime zest. Beat oil mixture into flour mixture with an electric mixer at medium speed until blended and smooth.

In a large bowl beat the egg whites with an electric mixer at high speed until foamy. Add cream of tartar, beating until soft peaks form. Gradually add remaining ¼ cup sugar, 1 tablespoon at a time, beating until stiff peaks form. Gently stir one-fourth of the egg white mixture into the flour mixture, then gently fold in remaining egg white mixture. Pour mixture into the prepared pans.

Bake 18–21 minutes or until cakes spring back when lightly touched. Cool in pans for 10 minutes on wire racks. Remove cakes from pans and cool completely on wire racks.

To prepare the frosting, whisk the powdered sugar and remaining 2 tablespoons lime juice in a large bowl. Fold in the whipped topping. Set aside.

Place 1 cake layer on a plate and spread half of the filling mixture. Top with second layer, remaining half of filling, and third cake layer. Spread frosting over top and sides of cake. Garnish with mint sprigs and lime wedges, if desired. Store cake loosely covered in refrigerator for up to 3 days. **Makes 16 servings.**

NUTRITION PER SERVING (1 SLICE):
CALORIES 259; FAT 6.3G (SAT 1.6G, MONO 2.9G, POLY 1.4G);
PROTEIN 4.5G; CHOLESTEROL 40.3MG; CARBOHYDRATE 29.7G.

Spiced Layer Cake

WITH CREAM CHEESE FROSTING

Molasses moistens the cake layers and adds another festive, fall flavor to this beautiful and delicious cake.

NONSTICK BAKING SPRAY WITH FLOUR

1 CUP SUGAR

⅓ CUP TRANS-FAT-FREE VEGETABLE SHORTENING (E.G., CRISCO® ZERO TRANS FAT SHORTENING)

1 TEASPOON VANILLA EXTRACT

3 LARGE EGGS

1¾ CUPS ALL-PURPOSE FLOUR

1½ TEASPOONS BAKING POWDER

1 TEASPOON GROUND GINGER

1 TEASPOON GROUND CARDAMOM

1 TEASPOON GROUND CINNAMON

1 TEASPOON GROUND NUTMEG

¼ TEASPOON SALT

¾ CUP 1% LOW-FAT MILK

¼ CUP MOLASSES

1 RECIPE CREAM CHEESE FROSTING (SEE PAGE 141)

Preheat oven to 350°F. Spray two 9-inch round cake pans with nonstick baking spray with flour.

In a large bowl beat the sugar, shortening, and vanilla with an electric mixer at medium speed until well blended (about 5 minutes). Add eggs, one at a time, beating well after each addition.

In a medium bowl whisk the flour, baking powder, ginger, cardamom, cinnamon, nutmeg, and salt. In a small bowl whisk the milk and molasses. Add the flour mixture to the sugar mixture alternately with the milk mixture, beginning and ending with the flour mixture. Pour batter into the prepared pans. Sharply tap pans once on counter to remove air bubbles.

Bake 28–30 minutes or until a wooden pick inserted in the center comes out clean. Cool in pans 10 minutes on a wire rack. Remove cakes from pans and cool completely on wire rack.

Prepare the Cream Cheese Frosting. Place 1 cake layer on a plate and spread with ½ cup frosting. Top with remaining cake layer. Spread remaining frosting over top and sides of cake. Chill 1 hour. Store cake loosely covered in refrigerator. **Makes 18 servings.**

NUTRITION PER SERVING (1 SLICE):
CALORIES 266; FAT 9.6G (SAT 3.5G, MONO 4.2G, POLY 1.5G);
PROTEIN 4.3G; CHOLESTEROL 50MG; CARBOHYDRATE 40.9G.

Mocha Buttercream Cake

Coffee cake layers, a mocha buttercream frosting, and chocolate-covered espresso beans add up to a terrific celebration cake for java junkies.

NONSTICK BAKING SPRAY WITH FLOUR	2 CUPS ALL-PURPOSE FLOUR
1¼ CUPS SUGAR	½ TEASPOON BAKING SODA
½ CUP (1 STICK) BUTTER, ROOM TEMPERATURE	½ TEASPOON SALT
2 TEASPOONS VANILLA EXTRACT	1 CUP FAT-FREE BUTTERMILK
1 TABLESPOON INSTANT ESPRESSO POWDER	1 RECIPE MOCHA BUTTERCREAM FROSTING (SEE PAGE 153)
2 LARGE EGGS	OPTIONAL: 16 CHOCOLATE-COVERED
1 LARGE EGG WHITE	ESPRESSO BEANS FOR GARNISH

Preheat oven to 350°F. Spray two 8-inch round cake pans with nonstick baking spray with flour. Set aside.

In a large bowl beat the sugar, butter, vanilla, and espresso powder with an electric mixer at medium speed until well blended (about 5 minutes). Add eggs and egg white, one at a time, beating well after each addition.

In a medium bowl whisk the flour, baking soda, and salt. Add the flour mixture to the sugar mixture alternately with buttermilk, beginning and ending with the flour mixture, beating well after each addition. Pour the batter into prepared pans.

Bake 23–26 minutes or until a wooden pick inserted in the center comes out clean. Cool in pans 10 minutes on a wire rack. Remove cakes from pans and cool completely on wire rack.

Prepare the Mocha Buttercream Frosting. Place 1 cake layer on a plate and spread with ⅓ cup frosting. Top with remaining cake layer. Spread remaining frosting over top and sides of cake. If desired, garnish outer edge of cake with chocolate-covered espresso beans. Store cake loosely covered in refrigerator. **Makes 16 servings.**

NUTRITION PER SERVING (1 SLICE):
CALORIES 286; FAT 10.8G (SAT 5.8G, MONO 4.3G, POLY 0.5G);
PROTEIN 4.9G; CHOLESTEROL 56.9MG; CARBOHYDRATE 41.7G.

Italian Cream Cake

The mellow flavor of toasted pecans, the tenderness of buttermilk cake and a generous swath of creamy frosting are all hallmarks of this remarkable dessert. Subtle and sophisticated in flavor, it will quickly become one of your favorites.

	NONSTICK BAKING SPRAY WITH FLOUR
2	CUPS SUGAR
6	TABLESPOONS (¾ STICK) BUTTER, ROOM TEMPERATURE
2	TABLESPOONS CANOLA OIL
2	LARGE EGG YOLKS
2	CUPS ALL-PURPOSE FLOUR
1	TEASPOON BAKING SODA
1	CUP FAT-FREE BUTTERMILK
½	CUP CHOPPED PECANS, LIGHTLY TOASTED
1	TEASPOON COCONUT EXTRACT
1	TEASPOON VANILLA EXTRACT
6	LARGE EGG WHITES, ROOM TEMPERATURE
1	RECIPE CREAM CAKE FROSTING (SEE PAGE 162)

Spray three 9-inch round cake pans with nonstick baking spray with flour.

In a large bowl beat the sugar, butter, and oil with an electric mixer at medium speed until well blended (about 5 minutes). Add egg yolks, one at a time, beating well after each addition.

In a medium bowl whisk the flour and baking soda. Add flour mixture to the butter mixture alternately with buttermilk, beginning and ending with the flour mixture. Stir in pecans, coconut extract, and vanilla.

In a large bowl beat the egg whites with an electric mixer at high speed until stiff peaks form. Fold egg whites into batter. Pour batter into the prepared pans.

Bake 22–24 minutes or until a wooden pick inserted in the center comes out clean. Let cool in pans 5 minutes on wire racks. Remove cakes from pans and cool completely on wire racks.

Prepare the Cream Cake Frosting. Place 1 cake layer on a plate and spread with ⅔ cup frosting. Top with another cake layer. Repeat with ⅔ cup frosting and remaining layer. Spread remaining frosting over top and sides of cake. **Makes 20 servings.**

NUTRITION PER SERVING (1 SLICE):
CALORIES 301; FAT 10G (SAT 4.2G, MONO 4.4G, POLY 1.3G);
PROTEIN 4.4G; CHOLESTEROL 40.7MG; CARBOHYDRATE 51G.

4. CUPCAKES

LEMONADE **CUPCAKES**, FAVORITE FUDGE **CUPCAKES**, VANILLA **CUPCAKES** WITH CHOCOLATE SOUR CREAM FROSTING, ELVIS **CUPCAKES**, ANGEL **CUPCAKES** WITH ANGEL FLUFF FROSTING, MAYAN CHOCOLATE **CUPCAKES**, BEE HAPPY HONEY **CUPCAKES**, COCOA CRÈME FRAÎCHE **CUPCAKES**, ROCKY ROAD **CUPCAKES**, CARROT **CUPCAKES** WITH LEMON BUTTERCREAM, RED VELVET **CUPCAKES**, GREEN TEA (MATCHA) **CUPCAKES**, RASPBERRY **CUPCAKES** WITH ORANGE BUTTERCREAM, VANILLA-GLAZED LAVENDER **CUPCAKES**, GINGER **CUPCAKES** WITH LIME FROSTING, SNOWBALL COCONUT **CUPCAKES**, CHAI **CUPCAKES** WITH WHITE CHOCOLATE CARDAMOM FROSTING, MOCHA **CUPCAKES** WITH ESPRESSO MERINGUE . . .

Lemonade Cupcakes

Petite and pretty, sweet and tart, these cupcakes have lots of lemon flavor and plenty of personality, too. They make an impressive summertime finale.

3½ CUPS CAKE FLOUR	2 LARGE EGG WHITES
2 TEASPOONS BAKING POWDER	1⅔ CUPS FAT-FREE MILK
¾ TEASPOON SALT	½ CUP PLAIN FAT-FREE YOGURT
½ TEASPOON BAKING SODA	2 TABLESPOONS FINELY GRATED LEMON ZEST
1¾ CUPS SUGAR	2 TEASPOONS LEMON EXTRACT
¼ CUP (½ STICK) UNSALTED BUTTER, ROOM TEMPERATURE	1 RECIPE LEMONADE FROSTING (SEE PAGE 143)
1½ TABLESPOONS CANOLA OIL	

Preheat oven to 350°F. Line 18 standard-size muffin cups with paper liners.

In a medium bowl whisk the flour, baking powder, salt, and baking soda.

In a large bowl beat the sugar, butter, and canola oil with an electric mixer at medium speed until well blended (about 5 minutes). Add egg whites, one at a time, beating well after each addition.

In a medium bowl whisk the milk, yogurt, lemon zest, and lemon extract until blended. Add flour mixture to the butter mixture alternately with the milk mixture, beginning and ending with the flour mixture. Spoon batter into the prepared cups.

Bake 17–20 minutes or until a wooden pick inserted in the center comes out clean. Cool in pans 10 minutes on wire racks. Remove cupcakes from pans. Cool completely on wire racks.

Prepare the Lemonade Frosting and frost the cupcakes. **Makes 18 cupcakes.**

NUTRITION PER SERVING (1 CUPCAKE):
CALORIES 299; FAT 6.7G (SAT 3.2G, MONO 2.7G, POLY 0.6G);
PROTEIN 4.3G; CHOLESTEROL 16.2MG; CARBOHYDRATE 57.4G.

Favorite Fudge Cupcakes

Sure, you can buy chocolate cake mix at the supermarket for your cupcakes, but they are easy to make from scratch. Plus, the results are yummier because you can use more cocoa powder and better ingredients. These favorite fudge cupcakes—cocoa cake and a swath of cocoa icing—are quick, rich, and delicious. Want proof? It's mere minutes away.

½ CUP UNSWEETENED COCOA POWDER (NOT DUTCH PROCESS)	⅓ CUP TRANS-FAT-FREE VEGETABLE SHORTENING (E.G., CRISCO® ZERO TRANS FAT SHORTENING)
½ CUP BOILING WATER	2 TEASPOONS VANILLA EXTRACT
2 CUPS CAKE FLOUR	2 LARGE EGGS
1 TEASPOON BAKING SODA	1 CUP FAT-FREE BUTTERMILK
½ TEASPOON SALT	1 RECIPE COCOA ICING (SEE PAGE 148)
1½ CUPS SUGAR	

Preheat oven to 350°F. Line 12 standard-size muffin cups with paper liners.

In a small bowl whisk the cocoa powder and boiling water until blended and smooth. Set aside to cool. In a medium bowl whisk the flour, baking soda, and salt.

In a large bowl beat the sugar, shortening, and vanilla with an electric mixer at medium speed until well blended. Add eggs, one at a time, beating well after each addition. Beat in the cocoa mixture until blended.

Add the flour mixture and buttermilk alternately to the sugar mixture, beginning and ending with the flour mixture and beating well after each addition. Spoon batter into the prepared cups.

Bake 15–18 minutes or until the cupcakes spring back when lightly touched.

Prepare the Cocoa Icing. Cool cupcakes in pan 10 minutes on a wire rack. Remove cupcakes from pan. Spread icing over cupcakes while they are still warm. **Makes 12 cupcakes.**

NUTRITION PER SERVING (1 CUPCAKE):
CALORIES 263; FAT 8.7G (SAT 1.7G, MONO 4.9G, POLY 2G);
PROTEIN 4.5G; CHOLESTEROL 38.8MG; CARBOHYDRATE 57.2G.

Cook's Note: Spreading the icing on the cupcakes while they are still warm helps the cupcakes stay extra moist.

Vanilla Cupcakes

WITH CHOCOLATE SOUR CREAM FROSTING

I have a yellowing newspaper clipping for "Classic Vanilla Cupcakes" that I saved when I was a teenager. It yields incredible cupcakes, but it also calls for a ton of sugar and an outrageous amount of butter. After much retooling, I've enlightened both the cakes and the accompanying frosting (one of my favorite frostings of all time, because it is so delicious and so easy). I think you'll love them as much as I do.

1¼ CUPS SUGAR	2 CUPS ALL-PURPOSE FLOUR
¼ CUP (½ STICK) BUTTER, ROOM TEMPERATURE	½ TEASPOON BAKING SODA
¼ CUP CANOLA OIL	½ TEASPOON SALT
2 TEASPOONS VANILLA EXTRACT	1 CUP FAT-FREE BUTTERMILK
2 LARGE EGGS	1 RECIPE CHOCOLATE SOUR CREAM FROSTING (SEE PAGE 150)
1 LARGE EGG WHITE	

Preheat oven to 350°F. Line 16 standard-size muffin cups with paper liners.

In a large bowl beat the sugar, butter, canola oil, and vanilla with an electric mixer at medium speed until well blended (about 5 minutes). Add the eggs and egg white, one at a time, beating well after each addition.

In a medium bowl whisk the flour, baking soda, and salt. Add the flour mixture to the sugar mixture alternately with the buttermilk, beginning and ending with the flour mixture, beating well after each addition. Spoon batter into the prepared cups.

Bake 16–18 minutes or until a wooden pick inserted in the center comes out clean. Cool in pans 10 minutes on a wire rack. Remove cupcakes from pans. Cool completely on wire rack.

Prepare the Chocolate Sour Cream Frosting and spread cupcakes with frosting. **Makes 16 cupcakes.**

NUTRITION PER SERVING (1 CUPCAKE):
CALORIES 300; FAT 10G (SAT 4G, MONO 4.6G, POLY 1.3G);
PROTEIN 4.3G; CHOLESTEROL 39.2MG; CARBOHYDRATE 49.7G.

Elvis Cupcakes

(BANANA CUPCAKES WITH PEANUT BUTTER FROSTING)

We all know that the King could sing, but he also purportedly loved a good fried banana-butter-peanut butter sandwich. In case you've never indulged, trust me when I say it is incredibly delicious. Unfortunately, the gooey concoction is also fatter than a herd of hogs. But no worries—you can savor the flavor, without anywhere near the fat, in these delectable cupcakes. Each is a hunka-hunka deliciousness.

1½ CUPS ALL-PURPOSE FLOUR

½ TEASPOON BAKING SODA

¼ TEASPOON SALT

1 CUP PACKED LIGHT BROWN SUGAR

¼ CUP (½ STICK) BUTTER, ROOM TEMPERATURE

2 LARGE EGGS

⅔ CUP MASHED RIPE BANANA (ABOUT 1 LARGE BANANA)

⅓ CUP PLAIN FAT-FREE YOGURT

1½ TEASPOONS VANILLA EXTRACT

1 RECIPE PEANUT BUTTER FROSTING (SEE PAGE 146)

Preheat oven to 350°F. Line 12 standard-size muffin cups with paper liners.

In a medium bowl whisk the flour, baking soda, and salt.

In a large bowl beat the brown sugar and butter with an electric mixer at medium speed until well blended. Add eggs, one at a time, beating well after each addition.

In a small bowl whisk the banana, yogurt, and vanilla until blended. Add the flour mixture to the butter mixture alternately with the banana mixture, beginning and ending with the flour mixture. Spoon batter into the prepared cups.

Bake 17–20 minutes or until a wooden pick inserted in the center comes out clean. Cool in pans 10 minutes on a wire rack. Remove cupcakes from pans. Cool completely on wire rack.

Prepare the Peanut Butter Frosting and frost the cupcakes. **Makes 12 cupcakes.**

NUTRITION PER SERVING (1 CUPCAKE):
CALORIES 295; FAT 9.8G (SAT 4.3G, MONO 3.9G, POLY 1.2G);
PROTEIN 6.2G; CHOLESTEROL 52.8MG; CARBOHYDRATE 46.7G.

Angel Cupcakes

WITH ANGEL FLUFF FROSTING

It's easy to take angel food cake for granted, layering it into trifles and tiramisu or as a base for strawberry shortcake. But this handheld interpretation makes it the star of the show, with a gloriously glossy frosting swirled on top (and yes, they really do have just 54 calories per serving— frosting included!). Be sure to try the variations, too, especially my favorite, pistachio-rose.

½ CUP CAKE FLOUR, SIFTED	1 TEASPOON VANILLA
¾ CUP SUGAR, DIVIDED USE	¾ TEASPOON FRESH LEMON JUICE
6 LARGE EGG WHITES, ROOM TEMPERATURE	1 RECIPE ANGEL FLUFF FROSTING (SEE PAGE
½ TEASPOON CREAM OF TARTAR	154)
⅛ TEASPOON SALT	

Preheat oven to 325°F. Line 24 standard-size muffin cups with paper liners.

In a small bowl whisk the flour and 6 tablespoons of the sugar.

In a large bowl beat the egg whites with an electric mixer at high speed until foamy. Add the cream of tartar and salt, beating until soft peaks form. Add the remaining 6 tablespoons sugar, 2 tablespoons at a time, beating until stiff peaks form. Beat in the vanilla and lemon juice.

Sift ¼ cup of the flour mixture over the egg white mixture, then fold in with a rubber spatula. Repeat procedure with remaining flour mixture. Spoon about 3 heaping tablespoons batter into each muffin cup.

Bake 13–15 minutes or until cupcakes spring back when lightly touched. Remove cupcakes from pans. Cool completely on wire racks.

Prepare the Angel Fluff Frosting and frost the cupcakes. **Makes 24 cupcakes.**

Variations

Chocolate-Chip Angel Cupcakes: Fold in ½ cup semisweet miniature chocolate chips after folding in the flour.

Pistachio Rose Angel Cupcakes: Replace the vanilla extract with ½ teaspoon of rose water. Fold in ½ cup chopped lightly salted, roasted, shelled pistachios after folding in the flour.

Lime Angel Cupcakes: Replace the lemon juice with an equal amount of lime juice and beat in 1 tablespoon finely grated lime zest with the lime juice and vanilla.

NUTRITION PER SERVING (1 CUPCAKE):
CALORIES 54; FAT 0G (SAT 0G, MONO 0G, POLY 0G);
PROTEIN 1.2G; CHOLESTEROL 0MG; CARBOHYDRATE 12.4G.

Mayan Chocolate Cupcakes

Because I'm testing recipes all day, most every day, I tend not to overindulge. That changed when I started testing these cupcakes: I found it extremely challenging to stop at one. They are so simple to prepare, too—the chocolate chips in the cake batter take the place of any frosting or icing.

⅔ CUP PACKED DARK BROWN SUGAR

⅔ CUP SUGAR

⅓ CUP TRANS-FAT-FREE VEGETABLE SHORT-
ENING (E.G., CRISCO® ZERO TRANS FAT
SHORTENING)

2 TEASPOONS VANILLA EXTRACT

3 LARGE EGGS

1 CUP WHOLE WHEAT PASTRY FLOUR (OR
ALL-PURPOSE FLOUR)

¾ CUP ALL-PURPOSE FLOUR

½ CUP UNSWEETENED COCOA POWDER (NOT
DUTCH PROCESS)

1 TEASPOON GROUND CINNAMON

½ TEASPOON CHIPOTLE CHILE POWDER

1 TEASPOON BAKING POWDER

1 TEASPOON BAKING SODA

½ TEASPOON SALT

1¼ CUPS FAT-FREE MILK

¾ CUP MINIATURE SEMISWEET CHOCOLATE
CHIPS

2 TABLESPOONS POWDERED SUGAR

Preheat oven to 350°F. Line 18 standard-size muffin cups with paper liners.

In a large bowl beat the brown sugar, sugar, shortening, and vanilla with an electric mixer at medium speed until well blended (about 5 minutes). Add the eggs, one at a time, beating well after each addition.

In a medium bowl whisk the flours, cocoa powder, cinnamon, chile powder, baking powder, baking soda, and salt. Add the flour mixture to the sugar mixture alternately with milk, beginning and ending with the flour mixture, beating well after each addition. Stir in the chocolate chips. Spoon batter into the prepared cups.

Bake 16–18 minutes or until a wooden pick inserted in the center comes out clean. Cool in pans 10 minutes on a wire rack. Remove cupcakes from pans. Cool completely on wire rack. Sprinkle cupcakes with powdered sugar. **Makes 18 cupcakes.**

NUTRITION PER SERVING (1 CUPCAKE):
CALORIES 163; FAT 5.3G (SAT 0.8G, MONO 2.8G, POLY 1.4G);
PROTEIN 3.3G; CHOLESTEROL 35.6MG; CARBOHYDRATE 26.9G.

Bee Happy Honey Cupcakes

I love this recipe as cupcakes, but I also like to bake it in small loaves—perfect for gift-giving. Mild honey lends sweetness, while brown sugar and vanilla add subtle notes of caramel.

¾	CUP ALL-PURPOSE FLOUR	5	TABLESPOONS UNSALTED BUTTER, ROOM TEMPERATURE
½	CUP WHOLE WHEAT PASTRY FLOUR (OR ALL-PURPOSE FLOUR)	2	LARGE EGGS
1¼	TEASPOONS BAKING POWDER	¼	CUP 1% LOW-FAT MILK
¼	TEASPOON GROUND CORIANDER OR NUTMEG	¼	CUP HONEY
¼	TEASPOON SALT	2	TEASPOONS VANILLA EXTRACT
½	CUP PACKED LIGHT BROWN SUGAR	1	RECIPE HONEY BUTTERCREAM FROSTING (SEE PAGE 159)

Preheat oven to 350°F. Line 12 standard-size muffin cups with paper liners.

In a medium bowl whisk the flours, baking powder, coriander and salt.

In a large bowl beat the brown sugar and butter with an electric mixer at medium speed until well blended (about 5 minutes). Add eggs, one at a time, beating well after each addition.

In a medium bowl whisk the milk, honey and vanilla until slightly blended. Add flour mixture to butter mixture alternately with the milk mixture, beginning and ending with the flour mixture. Spoon batter into the prepared cups.

Bake 13–17 minutes or until a wooden pick inserted in the center comes out clean. Cool in pans 10 minutes on wire racks. Remove cupcakes from pans. Cool completely on wire racks.

Prepare the Honey Buttercream Frosting and frost the cupcakes. **Makes 12 cupcakes.**

NUTRITION PER SERVING (1 CUPCAKE):
CALORIES 251; FAT 8.1G (SAT 3.9G, MONO 3.3G, POLY 0.4G);
PROTEIN 2.7G; CHOLESTEROL 54.3MG; CARBOHYDRATE 43.4G.

Cocoa Crème Fraîche Cupcakes

Authentic crème fraîche is a rich, thickened cream with slightly tangy, nutty flavor and velvety texture. It's easy to make a light delicious version at home with three ingredients. Besides making an ethereal frosting for these petite cocoa cakes, it is also delicious spooned over fresh fruit or other desserts such as warm pie, crisps, or cobblers.

1 CUP PACKED LIGHT BROWN SUGAR	1 TEASPOON BAKING POWDER
6 TABLESPOONS (¾ STICK) BUTTER, ROOM TEMPERATURE	½ TEASPOON BAKING SODA
	½ TEASPOON SALT
1 TEASPOON VANILLA EXTRACT	¾ CUP REDUCED-FAT SOUR CREAM, DIVIDED USE
¾ TEASPOON ALMOND EXTRACT, DIVIDED USE	
2 LARGE EGGS	1½ CUPS FROZEN FAT-FREE NON-DAIRY WHIPPED TOPPING, THAWED
1¼ CUPS ALL-PURPOSE FLOUR	
½ CUP UNSWEETENED COCOA POWDER (NOT DUTCH PROCESS)	

Preheat oven to 400°F. Line 18 standard-size muffin cups with paper liners.

In a large bowl beat the brown sugar, butter, vanilla, and ½ teaspoon of the almond extract with an electric mixer at medium speed until well blended. Add eggs, one at a time, beating well after each addition.

In a medium bowl whisk the flour, cocoa powder, baking powder, baking soda, and salt. With electric mixer on low speed, beat the flour mixture into the butter mixture alternately with ½ cup of the sour cream, beginning and ending with the flour mixture. Spoon batter into the prepared cups.

Bake 11–13 minutes or until cupcakes spring back when touched lightly in the center. Transfer pans to wire racks and cool 10 minutes. Remove cupcakes from pans. Cool completely on wire racks.

In a medium bowl whisk the whipped topping with the remaining ¼ teaspoon almond extract and the remaining ¼ cup sour cream until blended. Frost each cupcake with whipped topping mixture. Store in the refrigerator. **Makes 18 cupcakes.**

NUTRITION PER SERVING (1 CUPCAKE):
CALORIES 148; FAT 6G (SAT 3.4G, MONO 1.9G, POLY 0.3G);
PROTEIN 2.4G; CHOLESTEROL 35.9MG; CARBOHYDRATE 22G.

Rocky Road Cupcakes

This favorite trilogy of flavors—chocolate, marshmallow and nuts—makes a straightforward cupcake favorite.

1 CUP PACKED LIGHT BROWN SUGAR	1 TEASPOON BAKING SODA
1 LARGE EGG	½ TEASPOON BAKING POWDER
2 LARGE EGG WHITES	¼ TEASPOON SALT
⅓ CUP CANOLA OIL	1 CUP FAT-FREE BUTTERMILK
1 TEASPOON VANILLA EXTRACT	½ CUP MINIATURE SEMISWEET CHOCOLATE
¾ CUP ALL-PURPOSE FLOUR	CHIPS
¾ CUP WHOLE WHEAT PASTRY FLOUR (OR	2 CUPS MINIATURE MARSHMALLOWS
ALL-PURPOSE FLOUR)	⅓ CUP CHOPPED WALNUTS OR PECANS,
⅔ CUP UNSWEETENED COCOA POWDER (NOT	TOASTED
DUTCH PROCESS)	

Preheat oven to 350°F. Line 16 standard-size muffin cups with paper liners.

In a large bowl beat the brown sugar, egg, egg whites, canola oil, and vanilla with an electric mixer at medium speed until well blended (about 2 minutes).

In a medium bowl whisk the flours, cocoa powder, baking soda, baking powder, and salt. Stir the flour mixture into the sugar mixture alternately with buttermilk, beginning and ending with the flour mixture. Mix after each addition until just blended. Spoon batter into the prepared cups.

Bake 12 minutes. Open oven door and sprinkle tops of cupcakes with the chocolate chips, marshmallows, and walnuts. Continue baking 4–6 minutes longer or until a wooden pick inserted in the center of a cupcake comes out with moist crumbs attached (do not overbake). Cool in pans 10 minutes on a wire rack. Remove cupcakes from pans. Cool completely on wire rack. **Makes 16 cupcakes.**

NUTRITION PER SERVING (1 CUPCAKE):
CALORIES 196; FAT 7G (SAT 0.9G, MONO 3.8G, POLY 1.9G);
PROTEIN 3.5G; CHOLESTEROL 13.5MG; CARBOHYDRATE 32.1G.

Carrot Cupcakes

WITH LEMON BUTTERCREAM

Making multiple confections instead of one big layer cake lends favorite carrot cake extra charm and appeal.

⅔ CUP SUGAR	1 TEASPOON BAKING POWDER
3 TABLESPOONS CANOLA OIL	¾ TEASPOON GROUND CINNAMON
1 TEASPOON VANILLA EXTRACT	¼ TEASPOON BAKING SODA
1 LARGE EGG	⅛ TEASPOON SALT
1 CUP FINELY SHREDDED, PEELED CARROT (ABOUT 2 MEDIUM CARROTS)	⅛ TEASPOON GROUND NUTMEG
	⅓ CUP DRIED TART CHERRIES OR DRIED
1 8-OUNCE CAN CRUSHED PINEAPPLE, WELL-DRAINED	CRANBERRIES, COARSELY CHOPPED
1 CUP WHOLE WHEAT PASTRY FLOUR (OR ALL-PURPOSE FLOUR)	1 RECIPE LEMON BUTTERCREAM (SEE PAGE 145)

Preheat oven to 350°F. Line 12 standard-size muffin cups with paper liners.

In a large bowl beat the sugar, canola oil, vanilla, and egg with an electric mixer at medium speed until well blended. Stir in the carrot and pineapple.

In a medium bowl whisk the flour, baking powder, cinnamon, baking soda, salt and nutmeg. Stir the flour mixture into the sugar mixture until well blended (do not overmix). Stir in dried cherries. Spoon batter into the prepared cups.

Bake 16–18 minutes or until a wooden pick inserted in the center comes out clean. Cool in pan 10 minutes on a wire rack. Remove cupcakes from pan. Cool completely on wire rack.

Prepare the Lemon Buttercream and frost the cupcakes. **Makes 12 cupcakes.**

NUTRITION PER SERVING (1 CUPCAKE):
CALORIES 222; FAT 7G (SAT 2.1G, MONO 3.3G, POLY 1.2G);
PROTEIN 2.3G; CHOLESTEROL 26.3MG; CARBOHYDRATE 38.5G.

Red Velvet Cupcakes

Although most often credited to the American South, no definitive information exists on exactly where red velvet cake originated, how it should be made or why it is red. But this colorful and delicious cake (thanks in part to buttermilk and cocoa powder) is a winner, especially at Christmastime or on Valentine's Day.

1¼ CUPS SUGAR

⅓ CUP TRANS-FAT-FREE VEGETABLE SHORTENING (E.G., CRISCO® ZERO TRANS FAT SHORTENING)

2 LARGE EGG WHITES

1 LARGE EGG

1½ TEASPOONS VANILLA EXTRACT

1 TABLESPOON UNSWEETENED COCOA POWDER (NOT DUTCH PROCESS)

1 1-OUNCE BOTTLE RED FOOD COLORING

2 CUPS CAKE FLOUR

½ TEASPOON SALT

1 CUP LOW-FAT BUTTERMILK

1 TABLESPOON WHITE VINEGAR

1 TEASPOON BAKING SODA

1 RECIPE WHITE CHOCOLATE FROSTING (SEE PAGE 142)

Preheat oven to 350°F. Line 18 standard-size muffin cups with paper liners.

In a large bowl beat the sugar and shortening with an electric mixer at medium speed until well blended (about 5 minutes). Add egg whites, egg, and vanilla, beating well after each addition. Add the cocoa powder and red food coloring, beating until well blended.

In a medium bowl whisk the cake flour and salt. Add the flour mixture to the sugar mixture alternately with buttermilk, beginning and ending with the flour mixture. In a small cup combine the vinegar and baking soda, then add to batter, stirring well. Spoon batter into the prepared cups. Sharply tap pans once on counter to remove air bubbles.

Bake 15–18 minutes or until a wooden pick inserted in the center comes out clean. Cool in pans 10 minutes on wire racks. Remove cupcakes from pans. Cool completely on wire racks.

Prepare the White Chocolate Frosting and frost the cupcakes. Spread cupcakes with White Chocolate Frosting. **Makes 18 cupcakes.**

NUTRITION PER SERVING (1 CUPCAKE):
CALORIES 251; FAT 7.4G (SAT 2.4G, MONO 3.3G, POLY 1.4G);
PROTEIN 3G; CHOLESTEROL 17.6MG; CARBOHYDRATE 43.4G.

Green Tea (Matcha) Cupcakes

No doubt about it, these are fun, fantastic-tasting cupcakes. I like the flavor of the green tea to be fairly pronounced, but you can certainly play around with the amount of matcha (in both batter and frosting) to suit your taste. It's worth inviting some green tea-loving friends over to help make these, too, because making them is just as fun as eating them. The bright green batter (thanks to the matcha) makes you feel like you've just slipped into a Dr. Seuss story.

¼ CUP BOILING WATER	5 TABLESPOONS CANOLA OIL
2 TABLESPOONS MATCHA (INSTANT GREEN TEA POWDER)	2 TEASPOONS VANILLA EXTRACT
⅔ CUP LOW-FAT BUTTERMILK	2 LARGE EGGS
2½ CUPS ALL-PURPOSE FLOUR, SIFTED	3 LARGE EGG WHITES
1 TEASPOON BAKING SODA	1 RECIPE GREEN TEA BUTTERCREAM (SEE PAGE 163)
½ TEASPOON SALT	OPTIONAL: SMALL EDIBLE TROPICAL FLOWERS FOR GARNISH
1½ CUPS SUGAR	
5 TABLESPOONS BUTTER, ROOM TEMPERATURE	

Preheat oven to 350°F. Line 24 standard-size muffin cups with paper liners.

In a small cup combine boiling water and matcha, stirring until matcha dissolves. Cool, then stir in buttermilk.

In a medium bowl whisk the sifted flour, baking soda, and salt.

In a large bowl beat the sugar, butter, canola oil, and vanilla with an electric mixer at medium speed until well blended (about 5 minutes). Add eggs and egg whites, one at a time, beating well after each addition. Add flour mixture to butter mixture alternately with matcha mixture, beginning and ending with flour mixture. Spoon batter into the prepared muffin cups.

Bake 17–20 minutes or until a wooden pick inserted in the center comes out clean. Cool in pans 10 minutes on wire racks. Remove cupcakes from pans. Cool completely on wire racks.

Prepare the Green Tea Buttercream and frost the cupcakes. If desired, garnish with small tropical flowers. **Makes 24 cupcakes.**

NUTRITION PER SERVING (1 CUPCAKE):
CALORIES 232; FAT 6.1G (SAT 1.9G, MONO 2.8G, POLY 1G);
PROTEIN 3G; CHOLESTEROL 25.6MG; CARBOHYDRATE 42G.

Raspberry Cupcakes

WITH ORANGE BUTTERCREAM

These cupcakes taste like late summer: fresh and fragrant with fruit. You can make them with just about any ripe berry that suits your fancy, including blueberries, blackberries, and boysenberries. I strongly suggest serving them with some extra berries on top...I like a raspberry with every bite.

⅔ CUP ALL-PURPOSE FLOUR

1 CUP FRESH RASPBERRIES

⅔ CUP SUGAR

1½ TEASPOONS BAKING POWDER

¼ TEASPOON SALT

⅛ TEASPOON BAKING SODA

¼ CUP (½ STICK) BUTTER, MELTED

1 LARGE EGG

¾ CUP LOW-FAT BUTTERMILK

¼ CUP FAT-FREE MILK

2 TEASPOONS FRESH GRATED ORANGE ZEST

1 RECIPE ORANGE BUTTERCREAM (SEE PAGE 145)

OPTIONAL: FRESH RASPBERRIES AND SMALL FRESH MINT LEAVES

Preheat oven to 350°F. Line 12 standard-size muffin cups with paper liners.

Place the flour in a large bowl. Measure 1 tablespoon flour from the bowl and toss with the raspberries in a medium bowl.

Whisk the sugar, baking powder, salt, and baking soda into the large bowl with the flour. In a medium bowl whisk the melted butter, egg, buttermilk, milk, and orange zest until blended. Add buttermilk mixture to flour mixture, stirring just until moist. Fold raspberries into batter. Spoon batter into the prepared cups.

Bake 22–25 minutes or until a wooden pick inserted in the center comes out clean. Cool in pans 10 minutes on wire racks. Remove cupcakes from pans. Cool completely on wire racks.

Prepare the Orange Buttercream and frost the cupcakes. If desired, garnish with fresh raspberries and mint leaves. **Makes 12 cupcakes.**

NUTRITION PER SERVING (1 CUPCAKE):
CALORIES 249; FAT 8.1G (SAT 4.1G, MONO 3.1G, POLY 0.4G);
PROTEIN 3.8G; CHOLESTEROL 38.4MG; CARBOHYDRATE 40.9G.

Vanilla-Glazed Lavender Cupcakes

Lavender, coupled with vanilla (which originates from orchids), adds bewitching floral notes to these tender little cakes. You'll want to make them for bridal and baby showers (you can tint the icing pale pink or pale blue for the latter), or simply for your next cup of tea.

1 CUP SUGAR	¼ TEASPOON SALT
3 TABLESPOONS DRIED LAVENDER LEAVES	1 CUP LOW-FAT BUTTERMILK
5 TABLESPOONS UNSALTED BUTTER, ROOM TEMPERATURE	1⅓ CUPS SIFTED POWDERED SUGAR
½ TEASPOON VANILLA EXTRACT	2 TEASPOONS WATER
1 LARGE EGG	1 TEASPOON VANILLA EXTRACT
1 LARGE EGG WHITE	ONE TINY DROP EACH OF RED & BLUE FOOD
1¾ CUPS ALL-PURPOSE FLOUR	COLORING (TO TINT PALE LAVENDER)
1 TEASPOON BAKING POWDER	OPTIONAL GARNISH: SUGARED VIOLETS OR
¼ TEASPOON BAKING SODA	SMALL FRESH EDIBLE FLOWERS

Preheat oven to 350°F. Line 12 standard-size muffin cups with paper liners.

Process the sugar and lavender in small food processor. Transfer the lavender sugar to a large bowl. Add the butter and vanilla and beat with an electric mixer set at medium speed until well blended (about 5 minutes). Add egg and egg white, one at a time, beating well after each addition.

Whisk the flour, baking powder, baking soda, and salt in a small bowl. Add flour mixture to butter mixture alternately with buttermilk, beginning and ending with flour mixture. Spoon batter into the prepared cups.

Bake 17–20 minutes or until a wooden pick inserted in the center comes out clean. Cool in pans 10 minutes on wire racks.

While the cupcakes cool, combine powdered sugar, water, vanilla, and red and blue food coloring (use the tip of a toothpick to get a small drop of color into icing). Remove cupcakes from pan and spoon icing over warm cupcakes to cover. Cool completely on wire rack. If desired, garnish with sugared violets or edible flowers. **Makes 12 cupcakes.**

NUTRITION PER SERVING (1 CUPCAKE):
CALORIES 238; FAT 6.1G (SAT 2.9G, MONO 2.4G, POLY 0.3G);
PROTEIN 3.6G; CHOLESTEROL 32.7MG; CARBOHYDRATE 42.9G.

Ginger Cupcakes

WITH LIME FROSTING

Heady with sweet spices, these cupcakes fill all your senses and leave you longing for more. A big dose of lime (from lime juice and lime zest) in the frosting really makes these sing.

2½ CUPS ALL-PURPOSE FLOUR	¼ CUP CANOLA OIL
1½ TABLESPOONS GROUND GINGER	1 LARGE EGG
1 TEASPOON BAKING SODA	1 CUP DARK MOLASSES (NOT BLACKSTRAP)
1 TEASPOON GROUND CINNAMON	⅔ CUP LOW-FAT BUTTERMILK
1 TEASPOON GROUND ALLSPICE	¼ CUP CHOPPED CRYSTALLIZED GINGER
¼ TEASPOON SALT	1 RECIPE FRESH LIME FROSTING (SEE PAGE
½ CUP PACKED LIGHT BROWN SUGAR	144)

Preheat oven to 350°F. Line 16 standard-size muffin cups with paper liners.

In a medium bowl whisk the flour, ginger, baking soda, cinnamon, allspice, and salt.

In a large bowl beat the brown sugar, canola oil, and egg with an electric mixer at medium speed until well blended (about 2 minutes). Add molasses, beating well.

Add flour mixture to molasses mixture alternately with buttermilk, beginning and ending with flour mixture. Stir in crystallized ginger. Spoon batter into prepared cups.

Bake 17–20 minutes or until a wooden pick inserted in the center comes out clean. Cool in pans 10 minutes on wire racks. Remove cupcakes from pans. Cool completely on wire racks.

Prepare the Fresh Lime Frosting and frost the cupcakes. **Makes 16 cupcakes.**

NUTRITION PER SERVING (1 CUPCAKE):
CALORIES 264; FAT 7.2G (SAT 2.0G, MONO 3.5G, POLY 1.3G);
PROTEIN 2.9G; CHOLESTEROL 22.2MG; CARBOHYDRATE 47.6G.

Snowball Coconut Cupcakes

These cupcakes owe their whimsical moniker to a snow-white, creamy coconut frosting and a generous dusting of flaked coconut.

2 CUPS ALL-PURPOSE FLOUR	¾ CUP CANNED LITE COCONUT MILK
1 TEASPOON BAKING SODA	¾ CUP FAT-FREE BUTTERMILK
½ TEASPOON SALT	2 TEASPOONS VANILLA EXTRACT
¼ CUP (½ STICK) UNSALTED BUTTER, ROOM TEMPERATURE	1 TEASPOON COCONUT-FLAVORED EXTRACT
2 TABLESPOONS CANOLA OIL	1 RECIPE CREAMY COCONUT FROSTING (SEE PAGE 147)
1⅓ CUPS SUGAR	½ CUP FLAKED SWEETENED COCONUT
3 LARGE EGG WHITES	

Preheat oven to 350°F. Line 12 standard-size muffin cups with paper liners.

In a medium bowl whisk the flour, baking soda, and salt.

In a large bowl beat the butter, canola oil, and sugar with an electric mixer at medium speed until fluffy (about 5 minutes). Add egg whites, one at a time, beating well after each addition.

In a medium bowl whisk the coconut milk, buttermilk, vanilla, and coconut extract until blended. Add flour mixture to butter mixture alternately with coconut milk mixture, beginning and ending with flour mixture. Spoon batter into prepared cups.

Bake 18–20 minutes or until a wooden pick inserted into center comes out clean. Cool in pans 10 minutes on wire racks. Remove cupcakes from pans. Cool completely on wire racks.

Prepare the Creamy Coconut Frosting. Spread cupcakes with the frosting. Sprinkle cupcakes with coconut. **Makes 12 cupcakes.**

NUTRITION PER SERVING (1 CUPCAKE):
CALORIES 240; FAT 6.6G (SAT 2.5G, MONO 1.8G, POLY 1.9G);
PROTEIN 2.4G; CHOLESTEROL 25.1MG; CARBOHYDRATE 38.7G.

Chai Cupcakes

WITH WHITE CHOCOLATE CARDAMOM FROSTING

Warm up to these delicious cakes, enlivened with the beloved spices of India—cardamom, ginger, cloves, and cinnamon. The delicate yet powerful flavors pack an irresistible punch.

2⅔ CUPS ALL-PURPOSE FLOUR	3 LARGE EGGS
1½ TEASPOONS BAKING POWDER	⅔ CUP HONEY
1¼ TEASPOONS GROUND GINGER	3 TABLESPOONS UNSALTED BUTTER, MELTED
1¼ TEASPOONS GROUND CINNAMON	2½ TABLESPOONS CANOLA OIL
½ TEASPOON GROUND CARDAMOM	6 TABLESPOONS FAT-FREE MILK
¼ TEASPOON GROUND CLOVES	1 RECIPE WHITE CHOCOLATE CARDAMOM
½ TEASPOON SALT	FROSTING (SEE PAGE 142)
¾ CUP PACKED LIGHT BROWN SUGAR	

Preheat oven to 350°F. Line 18 standard-size muffin cups with paper liners.

In a medium bowl whisk the flour, baking powder, ginger, cinnamon, cardamom, cloves, and salt.

In a large bowl whisk the brown sugar and eggs until blended. Whisk in the honey, melted butter, and canola oil until well blended. Stir in half of flour mixture until just blended. Stir in the milk until blended. Add remaining flour mixture, and stir just until flour mixture is moist. Spoon batter into prepared cups.

Bake 17–20 minutes or until a wooden pick inserted in the center comes out clean. Cool in pans 10 minutes on wire racks. Remove cupcakes from pans. Cool completely on wire racks.

Prepare White Chocolate Cardamom Frosting and frost the cupcakes. **Makes 18 cupcakes.**

NUTRITION PER SERVING (1 CUPCAKE):
CALORIES 286; FAT 7.8G (SAT 3.3G, MONO 3.1G, POLY 0.9G);
PROTEIN 4.2G; CHOLESTEROL 46.1MG; CARBOHYDRATE 50.5G.

Mocha Cupcakes

WITH ESPRESSO MERINGUE

If you're an espresso fan (like me), this scrumptious concoction is sure to make your mouth water. Don't be afraid of the meringue frosting—it's easy to master and will surely become one of your tried-and-true favorites.

1 CUP SUGAR	½ TEASPOON GROUND CINNAMON
2 LARGE EGGS	½ TEASPOON BAKING POWDER
⅓ CUP CANOLA OIL	¼ TEASPOON SALT
1 TEASPOON VANILLA EXTRACT	1 CUP FAT-FREE BUTTERMILK
1½ CUPS ALL-PURPOSE FLOUR	3 LARGE EGG WHITES, ROOM TEMPERATURE
⅔ CUP UNSWEETENED COCOA POWDER (NOT DUTCH PROCESS)	1½ CUPS POWDERED SUGAR
2 TEASPOONS INSTANT ESPRESSO POWDER, DIVIDED USE	OPTIONAL: 1–2 TEASPOONS UNSWEETENED COCOA POWDER FOR SPRINKLING CUPCAKE TOPS
1 TEASPOON BAKING SODA	

Preheat oven to 350°F. Line 16 standard-size muffin cups with paper liners.

In a large bowl beat the sugar, eggs, oil, and vanilla with an electric mixer at medium speed until well blended (about 2 minutes).

In a medium bowl whisk the flour, cocoa powder, 1 teaspoon espresso powder, baking soda, cinnamon, baking powder, and salt. Stir the flour mixture into the sugar mixture alternately with buttermilk, beginning and ending with the flour mixture. Mix after each addition until just blended. Spoon batter into the prepared cups.

Bake 16–18 minutes or until a wooden pick inserted in the center of a cupcake comes out with moist crumbs attached (do not overbake). Transfer pan to wire rack and cool 5 minutes. Remove cupcakes from pan to wire rack. Cool completely.

Mix the egg whites, powdered sugar and remaining 1 teaspoon of espresso powder in a medium stainless steel bowl. Set the bowl over a saucepan of simmering water and heat the whites, whisking constantly, until hot to the touch (165°F). Transfer the mixture to the bowl of a standing electric mixer fitted with a whisk and beat at high speed until the meringue is stiff and glossy, about 5 minutes. (Note: beat 8 minutes if using a handheld mixer.)

Scoop half of the espresso meringue into a pastry bag fitted with a large (¾-inch) plain tip and pipe the meringue onto half of the cupcakes. Repeat with the remaining espresso meringue and cupcakes. If desired, sprinkle the meringue with cocoa powder. **Makes 16 cupcakes.**

NUTRITION PER SERVING (1 CUPCAKE):
CALORIES 192; FAT 5.7G (SAT 0.8G, MONO 3.1G, POLY 1.5G);
PROTEIN 3.7G; CHOLESTEROL 26.7MG; CARBOHYDRATE 33.6G.

5. CHEESECAKES

NEW YORK CHEESECAKE, SOUR CREAM CHEESECAKE, BLUEBERRY CHEESECAKE, TRIPLE-CHERRY CHEESECAKE, LEMON LOVER'S CHEESECAKE, SO VERY CHOCOLATE CHEESECAKE, MASCARPONE CHEESECAKE WITH BALSAMIC STRAWBERRIES, CARAMEL CHEESECAKE, ITALIAN RICOTTA CHEESECAKE, MOCHA ESPRESSO CHEESECAKE, CHOCOLATE CHIP—ORANGE CHEESECAKE, VERMONT MAPLE SYRUP CHEESECAKE, RED BERRIES CHEESECAKE, FRESH GINGER CHEESECAKE, WILDFLOWER HONE CHEESECAKE, BLACK-BOTTOM BANANA CHEESECAKE, CAPPUCCINO CHEESECAKE, SUNSHINE CITRUS CHEESECAKE, SPICED PUMPKIN CHEESECAKE, CRANBERRY-JEWELED CHEESECAKE WITH CHOCOLATE COOKIE CRUST, BOURBON-SPIKED SWEET POTATO CHEESECAKE, GERMAN CHOCOLATE CHEESECAKE . . .

New York Cheesecake

It only takes a little bit of investigation to discover that people have varying ideas of what constitutes "true" New York cheesecake. There does seem to be consensus about a few elements, though, namely that it should be high, firm, and dense, with a slight citrus flavor. My enlightened adaptation here has all of that, but with a fraction of the fat and calories. Serve it straight up or gussied up—with chocolate sauce, caramel sauce, or fresh fruit.

1½ CUPS GROUND REDUCED-FAT GRAHAM CRACKER CRUMBS	3 TABLESPOONS ALL-PURPOSE FLOUR
3 TABLESPOONS UNSALTED BUTTER, MELTED	1 TABLESPOON VANILLA EXTRACT
2 TABLESPOONS PLUS 1⅓ CUPS SUGAR, DIVIDED USE	2 TEASPOONS FINELY GRATED ORANGE ZEST
	1 TEASPOON FINELY GRATED LEMON ZEST
3 8-OUNCE PACKAGES FAT-FREE CREAM CHEESE, ROOM TEMPERATURE	¼ TEASPOON SALT
	5 LARGE EGGS
2 8-OUNCE PACKAGES ⅓-LESS-FAT CREAM CHEESE, ROOM TEMPERATURE	

Position rack in the center of oven and preheat to 350°F. Wrap double layer of heavy-duty foil around outside of 10-inch-diameter springform pan. Spray bottom and sides of pan with nonstick cooking spray.

Combine graham cracker crumbs, melted butter and 2 tablespoons of the sugar in a small bowl. Using a large square of wax paper, press evenly into bottom and 1 inch up sides of prepared pan. Bake crust 8 minutes. Transfer to rack and cool while preparing filling. Increase oven temperature to 500°F.

In a large bowl beat the cream cheeses with an electric mixer at high speed until smooth. Add the flour, vanilla, orange zest, lemon zest, salt, and remaining 1⅓ cups sugar, beating well. Add eggs, one at a time, beating well after each addition. Pour filling mixture into prepared crust.

Bake 7 minutes. Reduce oven temperature to 200°F (do not remove cheesecake from oven) and bake 45 minutes or until almost set (cheesecake is done when the center barely moves when pan is touched). Transfer cheesecake to a cooling rack and run a knife around outside edge. Cool to room temperature, then chill at least 8 hours. Release pan sides. Cut into wedges. **Makes 10 servings.**

NUTRITION PER SERVING (1 WEDGE):
CALORIES 219; FAT 9.5G (SAT 5.3G, MONO 3.1G, POLY 0.4G);
PROTEIN 10.3G; CHOLESTEROL 84.9MG; CARBOHYDRATE 23.1G.

Sour Cream Cheesecake

It's the combination of light sour cream with several varieties of cheeses—blended cottage cheese, light cream cheese, and fat-free cream cheese—that add up to this super-creamy cheesecake. It will have cheesecake lovers begging for seconds.

1 CUP REDUCED-FAT GRAHAM CRACKER CRUMBS (ABOUT 10 COOKIE SHEETS)	¼ TEASPOON GROUND NUTMEG
2 TABLESPOONS (¼ STICK) UNSALTED BUTTER, MELTED	1 8-OUNCE PACKAGE ⅓-LESS-FAT CREAM CHEESE, ROOM TEMPERATURE
5 TABLESPOONS PLUS 1 CUP SUGAR, DIVIDED USE	1 8-OUNCE PACKAGE FAT-FREE CREAM CHEESE, ROOM TEMPERATURE
1 8-OUNCE CONTAINER 2% LOW-FAT COTTAGE CHEESE	3 LARGE EGGS
4 TEASPOONS VANILLA EXTRACT, DIVIDED USE	1 LARGE EGG WHITE
½ TEASPOON SALT	1 16-OUNCE CONTAINER REDUCED-FAT SOUR CREAM

Position rack in the center of oven and preheat to 350°F. Spray bottom and sides of a 9-inch-diameter springform pan with nonstick cooking spray.

Combine graham cracker crumbs, melted butter, and 2 tablespoons of the sugar in a small bowl. Using a large square of wax paper, press evenly into bottom and 1 inch up sides of prepared pan. Bake crust 10 minutes. Transfer to rack and cool while preparing filling.

In the large bowl of a food processor combine the cottage cheese, 3 teaspoons vanilla, salt, and nutmeg. Process 1–2 minutes or until smooth. Add cream cheese; process until smooth. Add eggs and egg white, one at a time, pulsing after each addition until well blended. Add 1 cup of the sugar, pulsing just until blended. Pour filling mixture into prepared crust.

Bake 45–50 minutes or until almost set (cheesecake is done when the center barely moves when pan is touched.) Remove the cheesecake from oven and let stand 10 minutes. Increase oven temperature to 450°F.

In a medium bowl combine the sour cream, remaining 1 teaspoon vanilla, and remaining 3 tablespoons sugar until blended. Spoon and spread evenly over cheesecake. Bake 5 minutes. Transfer cheesecake to a cooling rack and run a knife around outside edge. Cool to room temperature, then chill at least 8 hours. Release pan sides. Cut into wedges. **Makes 12 servings.**

NUTRITION PER SERVING (1 WEDGE):
CALORIES 243; FAT 11.5G (SAT 6.5G, MONO 3.6G, POLY 0.5G);
PROTEIN 9.1G; CHOLESTEROL 78.3MG; CARBOHYDRATE 26.4G.

Blueberry Cheesecake

A smattering of blueberries in an extra-creamy, sour cream-vanilla filling coupled with a crunchy vanilla crust add up to a taste of a true American classic. And since fresh or frozen blueberries work equally well, this recipe can be made all year long.

56 REDUCED-FAT VANILLA WAFERS

1 TABLESPOON BUTTER, MELTED

2½ CUPS FRESH OR FROZEN (THAWED AND DRAINED) BLUEBERRIES

5 TABLESPOONS ALL-PURPOSE FLOUR, DIVIDED USE

3 8-OUNCE PACKAGE FAT-FREE CREAM CHEESE, ROOM TEMPERATURE

1 8-OUNCE PACKAGE ⅓-LESS-FAT CREAM CHEESE, ROOM TEMPERATURE

1⅓ CUPS SUGAR

3 LARGE EGGS

3 LARGE EGG WHITES

1 8-OUNCE CONTAINER REDUCED-FAT SOUR CREAM

1 8-OUNCE CONTAINER FAT-FREE SOUR CREAM

1 TABLESPOON VANILLA EXTRACT

Position rack in the center of oven and preheat to 400°F. Wrap double layer of heavy-duty foil around outside of 10-inch-diameter springform pan. Spray bottom and sides of pan with nonstick cooking spray.

Process the wafers in a food processor until finely ground. Add the melted butter and pulse until mixture resembles coarse meal. Using a large square of wax paper, press and compact crumbs onto bottom (not sides) of springform pan. Bake 10 minutes. Transfer to rack and cool while preparing filling. Reduce oven temperature to 375°F.

In a medium bowl toss the blueberries with 1 tablespoon of the flour; set aside. In a large bowl beat the cream cheeses with an electric mixer at high speed until smooth. Add the sugar, beating well. Add remaining 4 tablespoons flour, beating well. Add eggs and egg whites, one at a time, beating well after each addition. Beat in sour cream and vanilla. Fold in prepared blueberries. Pour filling mixture into crust.

Place springform pan in large roasting pan. Pour enough hot water into roasting pan to come 1 inch up sides of pan. Bake cheesecake 1 hour or until just set in the center and top is slightly puffed and golden brown, about 1 hour. Turn off oven; keep door closed. Let cheesecake stand in oven 1 hour.

Remove cheesecake from roasting pan. Transfer cheesecake to a cooling rack and run a knife around outside edge. Cool to room temperature. Chill at least 8 hours. Release pan sides. Cut into wedges. **Makes 18 servings.**

NUTRITION PER SERVING (1 WEDGE):
CALORIES 245; FAT 7.9G (SAT 3.9G, MONO 2.1G, POLY 0.3G); PROTEIN 10.2G; CHOLESTEROL 56MG; CARBOHYDRATE 34.5G.

Triple-Cherry Cheesecake

Expect applause and other forms of adulation when you unveil this gorgeous cherry dessert. It's the inclusion of three types of cherry in the topping—dried, frozen, and cherry jam—that amplifies the flavor of the cake.

¾ CUP DRIED TART CHERRIES	2 TABLESPOONS PLUS 1⅓ CUPS SUGAR, DIVIDED USE
1 1-POUND BAG FROZEN PITTED BING CHERRIES, THAWED, DRAINED, JUICE RESERVED	2 8-OUNCE PACKAGES FAT-FREE CREAM CHEESE, ROOM TEMPERATURE
½ CUP CHERRY JAM	2 8-OUNCE PACKAGES ⅓-LESS-FAT CREAM CHEESE, ROOM TEMPERATURE
1 TEASPOON ALMOND EXTRACT, DIVIDED USE	1¼ CUPS REDUCED-FAT SOUR CREAM
1 TABLESPOON CORNSTARCH	¼ CUP ALL-PURPOSE FLOUR
1 TABLESPOON WATER	2 TABLESPOONS FRESH LEMON JUICE
1 CUP REDUCED-FAT GRAHAM CRACKER CRUMBS	3 LARGE EGGS
1 TABLESPOON BUTTER, MELTED	2 LARGE EGG WHITES

Combine dried cherries and reserved juice from thawed cherries in medium saucepan. Bring to boil. Remove from heat. Cover; let steep 20 minutes. Mix cherry jam, ½ teaspoon of the almond extract, cornstarch, and a tablespoon water in small bowl to blend. Stir into dried cherry mixture. Add thawed cherries. Stir over medium heat until mixture boils and thickens, about 1 minute. Cool, then cover and chill until cold.

Position rack in the center of oven and preheat to 325°F. Wrap double layer of heavy-duty foil around outside of 9-inch-diameter springform pan. Spray bottom and sides of pan with nonstick cooking spray.

Combine graham cracker crumbs, melted butter, and 2 tablespoons of the sugar in a small bowl. Using a large square of wax paper, press and compact crumbs onto bottom (not sides) of springform pan. Bake 10 minutes. Transfer to rack and cool while preparing filling. Maintain oven temperature.

In a large bowl beat the cream cheeses and sour cream with an electric mixer at high speed until smooth. Add the flour, remaining 1⅓ cups sugar, lemon juice, and remaining ½ teaspoon almond extract, beating well. Add eggs and egg whites, one at a time, beating well after each addition. Pour filling mixture into prepared crust.

Place springform pan in large roasting pan. Pour enough hot water into roasting pan to come 1 inch up sides of pan. Bake 1 hour and 10 minutes or until almost set (cheesecake is done when the center barely moves when pan is touched). Remove cheesecake from roasting pan. Transfer cheesecake to a cooling rack and run a knife around outside edge. Cool to room temperature, then chill at least 8 hours. Release pan sides. Spoon cherry topping evenly over cake, leaving ½-inch border around edge. Cut into wedges. **Makes 18 servings.**

NUTRITION PER SERVING (1 WEDGE):
CALORIES 269; FAT 10G (SAT 5.8, MONO 3.0G, POLY 0.4G);
PROTEIN 8.7G; CHOLESTEROL 64.5MG; CARBOHYDRATE 36.9G.

Lemon Lover's Cheesecake

The following recipe is adapted from a cheese pie my mother makes often. A refreshing finish to a hearty meal, it's also a snap to prepare.

1   8-OUNCE PACKAGE FAT-FREE CREAM CHEESE, ROOM TEMPERATURE

4   OUNCES (½ OF AN 8-OUNCE PACKAGE) ⅓-LESS-FAT CREAM CHEESE, ROOM TEMPERATURE

¾   CUP PLUS 2 TABLESPOONS SUGAR, DIVIDED USE

2   LARGE EGGS

¼   CUP FRESH LEMON JUICE

1   TABLESPOON FINELY GRATED LEMON ZEST

2   TEASPOONS VANILLA EXTRACT, DIVIDED USE

1   PURCHASED REDUCED-FAT 9-INCH GRAHAM CRACKER CRUST

1   CUP REDUCED-FAT SOUR CREAM

Preheat oven to 350°F. Blend the cream cheeses, ¾ cup of the sugar, eggs, lemon juice, lemon zest, and 1 teaspoon of the vanilla extract in large bowl of a food processor until well blended and smooth. Pour filling mixture into prepared crust.

Bake 30–35 minutes until filling is just set. Cool cheesecake slightly. Maintain oven temperature.

In a small bowl combine sour cream, remaining 1 teaspoon vanilla, and remaining 2 tablespoons sugar until blended. Spread mixture evenly over cheesecake. Bake 10 minutes. Transfer to a cooling rack and cool completely. Chill at least 8 hours. Cut into wedges and serve. **Makes 8 servings.**

NUTRITION PER SERVING (1 WEDGE):
CALORIES 297; FAT 9.8G (SAT 5.9G, MONO 2.6G, POLY 0.4G);
PROTEIN 8.9G; CHOLESTEROL 77.5MG; CARBOHYDRATE 39.3G.

So Very Chocolate Cheesecake

A crunchy chocolate cookie crust, intense chocolate filling, and a final drizzle of chocolate create the taste of a true American classic. With about half the fat and calories of regular chocolate cheesecake, this is a chocoholic's—and cheesecake lover's—dream come true.

1 CUP CHOCOLATE COOKIE CRUMBS	4 8-OUNCE PACKAGES FAT-FREE CREAM
1⅓ CUPS PLUS 2 TABLESPOONS SUGAR,	CHEESE, ROOM TEMPERATURE
DIVIDED USE	1 8-OUNCE PACKAGE ⅓-LESS-FAT CREAM
1 TABLESPOON BUTTER, MELTED	CHEESE, ROOM TEMPERATURE
3 1-OUNCE SQUARES UNSWEETENED BAKING	3 TABLESPOONS ALL-PURPOSE FLOUR
CHOCOLATE, CHOPPED	2 TEASPOONS VANILLA EXTRACT
½ CUP UNSWEETENED COCOA POWDER (NOT	4 LARGE EGGS
DUTCH PROCESS)	1 CUP FAT-FREE CHOCOLATE FUDGE ICE
¼ CUP 1% LOW-FAT MILK	CREAM TOPPING

Position rack in the center of oven and preheat to 350°F. Spray bottom and sides of 9-inch-diameter springform pan with nonstick cooking spray.

Combine the cookie crumbs, 2 tablespoons of the sugar, and melted butter in a small bowl. Using a large square of wax paper, press evenly into bottom (not sides) of prepared pan. Bake crust 5 minutes. Transfer to rack and cool while preparing filling. Maintain oven temperature.

Place the chopped chocolate in a small microwave-safe bowl. Microwave on 50 percent power in 1-minute intervals, stirring until smooth. Whisk in the cocoa powder and milk until blended and smooth.

In a large bowl beat the cream cheeses with an electric mixer at high speed until smooth. Add the remaining 1⅓ cups sugar, flour, and vanilla, beating well. Add chocolate mixture, beating well. Add eggs, one at a time, beating well after each addition. Pour filling mixture into prepared crust.

Bake 1 hour and 10 minutes or until almost set (cheesecake is done when the center barely moves when pan is touched). Transfer cheesecake to a cooling rack and run a knife around outside edge. Cool to room temperature, then chill at least 8 hours. Release pan sides. Cut into wedges. Drizzle each wedge with fudge topping. **Makes 18 servings.**

NUTRITION PER SERVING (1 WEDGE):
CALORIES 273; FAT 9.2G (SAT 5.1G, MONO 2.9G, POLY 0.5G);
PROTEIN 11.7G; CHOLESTEROL 63.1MG; CARBOHYDRATE 39.5G.

Mascarpone Cheesecake

WITH BALSAMIC STRAWBERRIES

Hailing from Italy's Lombardy region, mascarpone cheese is the star of this cheesecake's filling. Sweet and buttery-smooth, this Italian cream cheese (readily available at most well-stocked grocery stores) imparts a velvety texture and smooth flavor to this otherwise light cheesecake. Balsamic strawberries make an easy, elegant accompaniment.

56	REDUCED-FAT VANILLA WAFERS	1½	CUPS SUGAR, DIVIDED USE
1	TABLESPOON UNSALTED BUTTER, MELTED	2	TEASPOONS VANILLA EXTRACT
3	8-OUNCE PACKAGES FAT-FREE CREAM CHEESE, ROOM TEMPERATURE	2	LARGE EGGS
		2	LARGE EGG WHITES
1	8-OUNCE PACKAGES ⅓-LESS-FAT CREAM CHEESE, ROOM TEMPERATURE	3	CUPS QUARTERED HULLED STRAWBERRIES (ABOUT 1 AND ½ 12-OUNCE BASKETS)
1	8-OUNCE CONTAINER MASCARPONE CHEESE, ROOM TEMPERATURE	2	TABLESPOONS BALSAMIC VINEGAR

Position rack in the center of oven and preheat to 400°F. Wrap double layer of heavy-duty foil around outside of 10-inch-diameter springform pan. Spray bottom and sides of pan with nonstick cooking spray.

Process the vanilla wafers in a food processor until finely ground. Add the melted butter and pulse until mixture resembles coarse meal. Using a large square of wax paper, press and compact crumbs onto bottom (not sides) of springform pan. Bake 10 minutes. Transfer to rack and cool while preparing filling. Reduce oven temperature to 350°F.

In a large bowl beat the cream cheeses, mascarpone, 1¼ cups of the sugar, and vanilla with an electric mixer at high speed until smooth. Add eggs and egg whites, one at a time, beating well after each addition. Pour filling mixture into prepared crust.

Place springform pan in large roasting pan. Pour enough hot water into roasting pan to come halfway up sides of springform pan.

Bake 1 hour and 10 minutes or until almost set (cheesecake is done when the center barely moves when pan is touched). Transfer cheesecake to a cooling rack and run a knife around outside edge. Cool to room temperature, then chill at least 8 hours.

Mix strawberries, remaining ¼ cup sugar, and balsamic vinegar in large bowl. Let stand at room temperature until juices form, about 30 minutes. Release pan sides from cake. Cut into wedges. Spoon strawberries alongside each wedge and serve. **Makes 18 servings.**

NUTRITION PER SERVING (1 WEDGE):
CALORIES 219; FAT 7.6G (SAT 3.8G, MONO 1.9G, POLY 0.3G);
PROTEIN 8.4G; CHOLESTEROL 42.2MG; CARBOHYDRATE 30.9G.

Caramel Cheesecake

No doubt about it, anything with caramel in it, on it, or around it, is just right by me. The filling itself has hints of caramel, thanks to pure vanilla extract and a splurge of dark brown sugar. The caramel is present again, drizzled on top of the finished cake, and accentuated by a delicate sprinkle of fleur de sel flakes.

1½ CUPS REDUCED-FAT GRAHAM CRACKER
   CRUMBS

1½ TABLESPOONS SUGAR

3 TABLESPOONS BUTTER, MELTED

3 8-OUNCE PACKAGES FAT-FREE CREAM
   CHEESE, ROOM TEMPERATURE

1 8-OUNCE PACKAGE ⅓-LESS-FAT CREAM
   CHEESE, ROOM TEMPERATURE

1⅓ CUPS FIRMLY PACKED DARK BROWN SUGAR

¼ CUP ALL-PURPOSE FLOUR

3 LARGE EGGS

2 LARGE EGG WHITES

½ CUP REDUCED-FAT SOUR CREAM

2 TEASPOONS VANILLA EXTRACT

½ TEASPOON SALT

1 CUP FAT-FREE CARAMEL ICE CREAM TOPPING

OPTIONAL: FLEUR DE SEL FLAKES (SEA SALT
   FLAKES)

Position rack in the center of oven and preheat to 350°F. Spray bottom and sides of a 10-inch-diameter springform pan with nonstick cooking spray.

Combine graham cracker crumbs, sugar and melted butter in a small bowl. Using a large square of wax paper, press evenly into bottom (not sides) of prepared pan. Bake crust 12 minutes. Transfer to rack and cool while preparing filling. Maintain oven temperature.

In a large bowl beat the cream cheeses with an electric mixer at high speed until smooth. Add the brown sugar and flour, beating well. Add eggs and egg whites, one at a time, beating well after each addition. Add the sour cream, vanilla, and salt, beating until just blended. Pour filling mixture into prepared crust.

Bake 1 hour or until edges are just set but middle trembles slightly (cheesecake will continue to set as it cools). Turn off oven and cool cheesecake in oven with oven door propped open about 6 inches until cooled completely, about 2 hours.

Transfer cheesecake to a cooling rack and run a knife around outside edge. Pour caramel topping over cheesecake, spreading evenly. Chill at least 8 hours. Release pan sides. Sprinkle with fleur de sel just before serving. Cut into wedges. **Makes 18 servings.**

NUTRITION PER SERVING (1 WEDGE):
CALORIES 262; FAT 7.4G (SAT 3.9G, MONO 2.5G, POLY 0.3G);
PROTEIN 8.9G; CHOLESTEROL 55.7MG; CARBOHYDRATE 41.6G.

Italian Ricotta Cheesecake

Cream cheese complements ricotta in this luscious dessert and makes for a smooth, not grainy, filling.

1½ CUPS REDUCED-FAT GRAHAM CRACKER CRUMBS	2 8-OUNCE PACKAGES FAT-FREE CREAM CHEESE, ROOM TEMPERATURE
¼ TEASPOON GROUND NUTMEG	¼ CUP HONEY
1½ TABLESPOONS PLUS ¾ CUP SUGAR, DIVIDED USE	1 TABLESPOON FINELY GRATED ORANGE ZEST
3 TABLESPOONS BUTTER, MELTED	2 TEASPOONS VANILLA EXTRACT
1 15-OUNCE CONTAINER LOW-FAT RICOTTA	3 LARGE EGGS
	2 LARGE EGG WHITES

Position rack in the center of oven and preheat to 350°F. Wrap double layer of heavy-duty foil around outside of 10-inch-diameter springform pan. Spray bottom and sides of pan with nonstick cooking spray.

Combine graham cracker crumbs, nutmeg, 1½ tablespoons of the sugar, and melted butter in a small bowl. Using a large square of wax paper, press evenly into bottom (not sides) of prepared pan. Bake crust 12 minutes. Transfer to rack and cool while preparing filling. Maintain oven temperature.

Blend the ricotta in the bowl of a large food processor until smooth. Add the cream cheese and remaining ¾ cup sugar and blend well, stopping the machine occasionally and scraping down the sides of the bowl. Blend in the honey, orange zest, and vanilla. Add the eggs and egg whites, one at a time, pulsing just until blended. Pour filling mixture into prepared crust.

Place the springform pan in a large roasting pan. Pour enough hot water into the roasting pan to come halfway up the sides of the springform pan.

Bake 1 hour and 5 minutes or until almost set (cheesecake is done when the center barely moves when pan is touched). Transfer cheesecake to a cooling rack and run a knife around outside edge. Cool to room temperature, then chill at least 8 hours. Release pan sides. Cut into wedges. **Makes 16 servings.**

NUTRITION PER SERVING (1 WEDGE):
CALORIES 175; FAT 5.3G (SAT 2.6G, MONO 1.8G, POLY 0.3G);
PROTEIN 9.4G; CHOLESTEROL 57.2MG; CARBOHYDRATE 23.8G.

Mocha Espresso Cheesecake

It's easy to become addicted to this robust mocha cheesecake, sandwiched between a chocolate crust and chocolate fudge topping. Each bite belies its reduced-fat, reduced-calorie profile.

1½ CUPS REDUCED-FAT CHOCOLATE WAFER CRUMBS (ABOUT 50 COOKIES)

3 TABLESPOONS UNSALTED BUTTER, MELTED

1⅓ CUPS PLUS 2 TABLESPOONS SUGAR, DIVIDED USE

2 TABLESPOONS INSTANT ESPRESSO POWDER

1 TABLESPOON VANILLA EXTRACT

⅔ CUP UNSWEETENED COCOA POWDER (NOT DUTCH PROCESS)

¾ CUP REDUCED-FAT SOUR CREAM

2 8-OUNCE PACKAGES FAT-FREE CREAM CHEESE, ROOM TEMPERATURE

12 OUNCES ⅓-LESS-FAT CREAM CHEESE (1½ 8-OUNCE PACKAGES), ROOM TEMPERATURE

3 TABLESPOONS ALL-PURPOSE FLOUR

2 LARGE EGGS

2 LARGE EGG WHITES

⅔ CUP FAT-FREE CHOCOLATE FUDGE ICE CREAM TOPPING

Position rack in the center of oven and preheat to 350°F. Spray bottom and sides of a 9-inch-diameter springform pan with nonstick cooking spray.

In a small bowl combine cookie crumbs, melted butter, and 2 tablespoons sugar. Using a large square of wax paper, press evenly into bottom and 1 inch up sides of prepared pan. Bake crust 8 minutes. Transfer to rack and cool while preparing filling. Maintain oven temperature.

Stir together espresso powder and vanilla in a small bowl, stirring until espresso powder is dissolved. Whisk in the cocoa powder and sour cream; set aside. In a large bowl beat the cream cheeses with an electric mixer at high speed until smooth. Add the flour and remaining 1⅓ cups sugar, beating well. Add eggs and egg whites, one at a time, beating well after each addition. Add sour cream mixture, beating until just blended. Pour filling mixture into prepared crust.

Bake 1 hour and 5 minutes or until almost set (cheesecake is done when the center barely moves when pan is touched). Transfer cheesecake to a cooling rack and run a knife around outside edge. Cool to room temperature. Spread or decoratively drizzle chocolate topping over cheesecake Chill at least 8 hours. Release pan sides. Cut into wedges. **Makes 18 servings.**

NUTRITION PER SERVING (1 WEDGE):
CALORIES 295; FAT 10.1G (SAT 5.5G, MONO 3.4G, POLY 0.5G);
PROTEIN 8.8G; CHOLESTEROL 47.5MG; CARBOHYDRATE 44.5G.

Chocolate Chip-Orange Cheesecake

Chocolate, liqueur, and orange star in this very rich, very elegant cheesecake.

1   CUP REDUCED-FAT CHOCOLATE WAFER
    CRUMBS (ABOUT 33 COOKIES)

1   CUP PLUS 2 TABLESPOONS SUGAR,
    DIVIDED USE

1   TABLESPOON UNSALTED BUTTER, MELTED

3   8-OUNCE PACKAGES FAT-FREE CREAM
    CHEESE, ROOM TEMPERATURE

1   8-OUNCE PACKAGE ⅓-LESS-FAT CREAM
    CHEESE, ROOM TEMPERATURE

3   TABLESPOONS ALL-PURPOSE FLOUR

3   TABLESPOONS ORANGE LIQUEUR (SUCH AS
    GRAND MARNIER)

5   TEASPOONS FINELY GRATED ORANGE ZEST

2   TEASPOONS VANILLA EXTRACT

4   LARGE EGGS

¾   CUP MINIATURE SEMISWEET CHOCOLATE
    CHIPS

Position rack in the center of oven and preheat to 300°F. Spray bottom and sides of 10-inch-diameter springform pan with nonstick cooking spray.

Combine cookie crumbs, 2 tablespoons of the sugar and melted butter in a small bowl. Using a large square of wax paper, press and compact crumbs onto bottom (not sides) of springform pan. Bake 8 minutes. Transfer to rack and cool while preparing filling. Maintain oven temperature.

In a large bowl beat the cream cheeses with an electric mixer at high speed until smooth. Add the flour, liqueur, orange zest, vanilla, and remaining 1 cup sugar, beating well. Add eggs, one at a time, beating well after each addition. Stir in chocolate chips. Pour filling mixture into prepared crust.

Bake 1 hour or until almost set (cheesecake is done when the center barely moves when pan is touched). Transfer cheesecake to a cooling rack and run a knife around outside edge. Cool to room temperature, then chill at least 8 hours. Release pan sides. Cut into wedges. **Makes 16 servings.**

NUTRITION PER SERVING (1 WEDGE):
CALORIES 223; FAT 6.9G (SAT 3.5G, MONO 2.3G, POLY 0.5G);
PROTEIN 10.3G; CHOLESTEROL 68.2MG; CARBOHYDRATE 28.8G.

Vermont Maple Syrup Cheesecake

Embrace the flavors of fall in New England with this luscious take on a classic. The pure maple syrup infuses just the right amount of sweetness, creating a flavorful, heady treat.

56 REDUCED-FAT VANILLA WAFERS

1 TABLESPOON UNSALTED BUTTER, MELTED

3 8-OUNCE PACKAGES FAT-FREE CREAM CHEESE, ROOM TEMPERATURE

1 8-OUNCE PACKAGE ⅓-LESS-FAT CREAM CHEESE, ROOM TEMPERATURE

1 CUP PURE MAPLE SYRUP (PREFERABLY GRADE B)

4 LARGE EGGS

1 TABLESPOON VANILLA EXTRACT

½ CUP FAT-FREE EVAPORATED MILK

OPTIONAL: ADDITIONAL PURE MAPLE SYRUP FOR DRIZZLING

Position rack in the center of oven and preheat to 400°F. Spray bottom and sides of 10-inch-diameter springform pan with nonstick cooking spray.

Process the vanilla wafers in a food processor until finely ground. Add the melted butter and pulse until mixture resembles coarse meal. Using a large square of wax paper, press and compact crumbs onto bottom (not sides) of springform pan. Bake 10 minutes. Transfer to rack and cool while preparing filling. Reduce oven temperature to 350°F.

In a large bowl beat the cream cheeses with an electric mixer at high speed until smooth. Add the maple syrup, beating well. Add eggs, one at a time, beating well after each addition. Add vanilla and evaporated milk, beating until just blended. Pour filling mixture into prepared crust.

Bake 1 hour and 10 minutes or until almost set (cheesecake is done when the center barely moves when pan is touched). Transfer cheesecake to a cooling rack and run a knife around outside edge. Cool to room temperature, then chill at least 8 hours. Release pan sides. Cut into wedges. If desired, drizzle with additional maple syrup. **Makes 16 servings.**

NUTRITION PER SERVING (1 WEDGE):
CALORIES 218; FAT 7.4G (SAT 3.5G, MONO 1.9G, POLY 0.3G);
PROTEIN 10.1G; CHOLESTEROL 68.9MG; CARBOHYDRATE 27.6G.

Red Berries Cheesecake

Whipping the egg whites to soft peaks before folding them in makes this cheesecake very light and fluffy, unlike more traditional cheesecakes, which are creamy and dense. Do try the addition of rose water. It lends a subtle floral flavor that melds beautifully with the tart-sweet berries.

1 TABLESPOON UNSALTED BUTTER, ROOM TEMPERATURE	1¼ CUPS SUGAR, DIVIDED USE
⅔ CUP COARSELY GROUND REDUCED-FAT GRAHAM CRACKER CRUMBS	OPTIONAL: 1 TABLESPOON ROSE WATER
	4 LARGE EGG WHITES
2 8-OUNCE PACKAGES FAT-FREE CREAM CHEESE, ROOM TEMPERATURE	1 16-OUNCE CONTAINER REDUCED-FAT SOUR CREAM
1 8-OUNCE PACKAGES ⅓-LESS-FAT CREAM CHEESE, ROOM TEMPERATURE	1 PINT FRESH RASPBERRIES
	1 PINT FRESH STRAWBERRIES, HULLED AND SLICED

Position rack in the center of oven and preheat to 350°F. Spray bottom and sides of a 9-inch-diameter springform pan with nonstick cooking spray.

Spread butter evenly over bottom of prepared pan. Sprinkle with graham cracker crumbs. Bake in oven for 8 minutes to toast crumbs. Transfer to rack and cool while preparing filling. Maintain oven temperature.

In a large bowl beat the cream cheeses with an electric mixer at high speed until smooth. Add 1 cup of the sugar and the rose water (if using), beating well. Using electric mixer fitted with clean dry beaters, beat egg whites in another large bowl until stiff but not dry. Gently fold beaten whites into cheese mixture in 3 additions. Pour filling mixture into prepared crust.

Bake 35 minutes until filling is puffed and cracks begin to form around edges. Combine sour cream and remaining ¼ cup sugar in small bowl and stir until well blended. Spoon and spread mixture evenly over cake.

Bake cheesecake 5 minutes longer. Transfer cheesecake to a cooling rack and run a knife around outside edge. Cool to room temperature, then chill at least 8 hours. Release pan sides. Cut into wedges and serve with the raspberries and strawberries. **Makes 16 servings.**

NUTRITION PER SERVING (1 WEDGE):
CALORIES 201; FAT 8.3G (SAT 4.9G, MONO 2.5G, POLY 0.4G);
PROTEIN 7.6G; CHOLESTEROL 26.6MG; CARBOHYDRATE 24.9G.

Fresh Ginger Cheesecake

Between the spice-infused filling, made from a generous amount of fresh ginger, the crisp ginger-snappy crust, and the blanket of vanilla-ginger sour cream on top, this is a ginger connoisseur's delight.

1½ CUPS GINGERSNAP COOKIE CRUMBS	⅛ TEASPOON SALT
3 TABLESPOONS UNSALTED BUTTER, MELTED	3 TABLESPOONS MINCED PEELED FRESH GINGER
2 8-OUNCE PACKAGES FAT-FREE CREAM CHEESE, ROOM TEMPERATURE	3 LARGE EGGS
1 8-OUNCE PACKAGE ⅓-LESS-FAT CREAM CHEESE, ROOM TEMPERATURE	2 LARGE EGG WHITES
1¼ CUPS SUGAR, DIVIDED USE	1 16-OUNCE CONTAINER REDUCED-FAT SOUR CREAM
3 TEASPOONS VANILLA EXTRACT, DIVIDED USE	1 TEASPOON GROUND GINGER

Position rack in the center of oven and preheat to 350°F. Spray bottom and sides of a 9-inch-diameter springform pan with nonstick cooking spray.

Combine cookie crumbs and melted butter in a small bowl. Using a large square of wax paper, press evenly into bottom (not sides) of the prepared pan. Bake crust 10 minutes. Transfer to rack and cool while preparing filling. Maintain oven temperature.

In a large bowl beat the cream cheeses with an electric mixer at high speed until smooth. Add 1 cup of the sugar, 2 teaspoons of the vanilla, salt, and fresh ginger, beating well. Add eggs and egg whites, one at a time, beating well after each addition. Pour filling mixture into prepared crust.

Bake 15 minutes. Cover top of pan loosely with foil. Continue to bake cheesecake until sides begin to puff and center is softly set, about 50 minutes longer. Transfer to a cooling rack, uncover, and let stand 5 minutes. Maintain oven temperature.

In a medium bowl whisk the sour cream, ground ginger, remaining ¼ cup sugar and remaining 1 teaspoon vanilla. Spoon and spread evenly over cake. Return to oven and bake 10 minutes. Transfer cheesecake to a cooling rack and run a knife around outside edge. Cool to room temperature, then chill at least 8 hours. Release pan sides. Cut into wedges. **Makes 18 servings.**

NUTRITION PER SERVING (1 WEDGE):
CALORIES 208; FAT 9.9G (SAT 5.5G, MONO 3.1G, POLY 0.4G);
PROTEIN 7.8G; CHOLESTEROL 62.1MG; CARBOHYDRATE 22.1G.

Wildflower Honey Cheesecake

This is loosely based on a traditional Greek cheesecake recipe served at one of my favorite restaurants in college. The orange flower water, a perfumy distillation of bitter-orange blossoms, sends the cheesecake to a whole new level. It is available at liquor stores or the baking section of some supermarkets.

1½ CUPS REDUCED-FAT GRAHAM CRACKER CRUMBS

1½ TABLESPOONS SUGAR

3 TABLESPOONS UNSALTED BUTTER, MELTED

3 8-OUNCE PACKAGES FAT-FREE CREAM CHEESE, ROOM TEMPERATURE

1 8-OUNCE PACKAGE ⅓-LESS-FAT CREAM CHEESE, ROOM TEMPERATURE

1 CUP WILDFLOWER HONEY

½ CUP REDUCED-FAT SOUR CREAM

OPTIONAL: 2½ TEASPOONS ORANGE FLOWER WATER

4 LARGE EGGS

OPTIONAL: HONEY FOR DRIZZLING

Position rack in the center of oven and preheat to 350°F. Spray bottom and sides of a 10-inch-diameter springform pan with nonstick cooking spray.

Combine graham cracker crumbs, sugar and melted butter in a small bowl. Using a large square of wax paper, press evenly into bottom (not sides) of prepared pan. Bake crust 12 minutes. Transfer to rack and cool while preparing filling. Maintain oven temperature.

In a large bowl beat the cream cheeses with an electric mixer at high speed until smooth. Add the honey, sour cream, and orange flower water (if using), beating well. Add eggs, one at a time, beating well after each addition. Pour filling mixture into prepared crust.

Bake 1 hour and 10 minutes or until almost set (cheesecake is done when the center barely moves when pan is touched). Transfer cheesecake to a cooling rack and run a knife around outside edge. Cool to room temperature, then chill at least 8 hours. Release pan sides. Cut into wedges. If desired, drizzle each wedge with additional honey. **Makes 18 servings.**

NUTRITION PER SERVING (1 WEDGE):
CALORIES 196; FAT 7.4G (SAT 3.9G, MONO 2.5G, POLY 0.4G);
PROTEIN 8.9G; CHOLESTEROL 66.9MG; CARBOHYDRATE 24.3G.

Black-Bottom Banana Cheesecake

Layers of chocolate crust, chocolate chips and a banana cream cheese filling make a stunning black-and-white combination for this indulgent cheesecake.

1	CUP REDUCED-FAT CHOCOLATE WAFER CRUMBS (ABOUT 33 COOKIES)	1	8-OUNCE PACKAGE ⅓-LESS-FAT CREAM CHEESE, ROOM TEMPERATURE
2	TABLESPOONS PLUS 1 CUP SUGAR, DIVIDED USE	1	8-OUNCE CONTAINER REDUCED-FAT SOUR CREAM
1	TABLESPOON UNSALTED BUTTER, MELTED	1½	CUPS MASHED RIPE BANANA
½	CUP MINIATURE SEMISWEET CHOCOLATE CHIPS	3	TABLESPOONS ALL-PURPOSE FLOUR
		2	TEASPOONS VANILLA EXTRACT
3	8-OUNCE PACKAGES FAT-FREE CREAM CHEESE, ROOM TEMPERATURE	3	LARGE EGGS
		2	LARGE EGG WHITES

Position rack in the center of oven and preheat to 325°F. Spray bottom and sides of a 9-inch-diameter springform pan with nonstick cooking spray.

Combine cookie crumbs, 2 tablespoons of the sugar, and melted butter in a small bowl. Using a large square of wax paper, press evenly into bottom (not sides) of prepared pan. Bake crust 5 minutes. Remove from oven and evenly sprinkle crust with chocolate chips. Bake 3 minutes longer. Transfer to rack and cool while preparing filling. Maintain oven temperature.

In a large bowl beat the cream cheeses and sour cream with an electric mixer at high speed until smooth. Add the remaining 1 cup sugar, mashed banana, flour, and vanilla, beating well. Add eggs and egg whites, one at a time, beating well after each addition. Pour filling mixture into prepared crust.

Bake 1 hour and 10 minutes or until almost set (cheesecake is done when the center barely moves when pan is touched). Transfer cheesecake to a cooling rack and run a knife around outside edge. Cool to room temperature, then chill at least 8 hours. Release pan sides. Cut into wedges. **Makes 18 servings.**

NUTRITION PER SERVING (1 WEDGE):
CALORIES 220; FAT 7.6G (SAT 4.1G, MONO 2.4G, POLY 0.5G);
PROTEIN 9.5G; CHOLESTEROL 54MG; CARBOHYDRATE 28.8G.

Cappuccino Cheesecake

Imagine that perfect cappuccino from your favorite coffeehouse transformed into an irresistible cheesecake. Exceptionally delicious, this creamy delicacy will become a fast favorite.

1½ CUPS REDUCED-FAT CHOCOLATE WAFER
   CRUMBS (ABOUT 50 COOKIES)
2 TABLESPOONS SUGAR
3 TABLESPOONS UNSALTED BUTTER, MELTED
2 TABLESPOONS INSTANT ESPRESSO POWDER
1 TEASPOON VANILLA EXTRACT
1 TABLESPOON WATER
2 8-OUNCE PACKAGES FAT-FREE CREAM
   CHEESE, ROOM TEMPERATURE

2 8-OUNCE PACKAGES ⅓-LESS-FAT CREAM
   CHEESE, ROOM TEMPERATURE
1 CUP PACKED LIGHT BROWN SUGAR
3 TABLESPOONS ALL-PURPOSE FLOUR
½ TEASPOON GROUND CINNAMON
2 LARGE EGGS
2 LARGE EGG WHITES
1 CUP FAT-FREE CHOCOLATE FUDGE ICE
   CREAM TOPPING, DIVIDED USE

Position rack in the center of oven and preheat to 425°F. Spray bottom and sides of 9-inch-diameter springform pan with nonstick cooking spray.

Combine cookie crumbs, sugar, and melted butter in a small bowl. Using a large square of wax paper, press evenly into bottom (not sides) of prepared pan. Bake crust 12 minutes. Transfer to rack and cool while preparing filling. Increase oven temperature to 450°F.

In a small cup combine the espresso powder, vanilla, and water, stirring to dissolve. In a large bowl beat the cream cheeses with an electric mixer at high speed until smooth. Add the brown sugar, flour, cinnamon, and espresso mixture, blending well. Add eggs and egg whites, one at a time, beating well after each addition. Pour filling mixture into prepared crust. Scoop 6 spoonfuls of fudge topping (1½ tablespoons each) onto cheesecake mixture. Swirl into batter using a knife.

Bake 10 minutes. Reduce oven temperature to 250°F (do not remove cheesecake from oven) and bake 1 hour or until almost set (cheesecake is done when the center barely moves when pan is touched). Transfer cheesecake to a cooling rack and run a knife around outside edge. Cool to room temperature, then chill at least 8 hours. Release pan sides. Cut into wedges. Serve with remaining chocolate topping. **Makes 18 servings.**

NUTRITION PER SERVING (1 WEDGE):
CALORIES 284.6; FAT 10.1G (SAT 5.6G, MONO 3.3G, POLY 0.6G);
PROTEIN 8.6G; CHOLESTEROL 48.7MG; CARBOHYDRATE 40.1G.

Sunshine Citrus Cheesecake

Fresh orange—both juice and zest—and fresh ginger enhance the creamy cheesecake filling in this treat. A crisp, gingery crust provides a delicious "snap."

1½ CUPS GROUND GINGERSNAP COOKIES

3   TABLESPOONS (¾ STICK) UNSALTED
    BUTTER, MELTED

4   TEASPOONS FINELY GRATED ORANGE ZEST,
    DIVIDED USE

1½ CUPS FRESH ORANGE JUICE

⅓ CUP ROUGHLY CHOPPED UNPEELED FRESH
    GINGER

3   8-OUNCE PACKAGES FAT-FREE CREAM
    CHEESE, ROOM TEMPERATURE

1   8-OUNCE PACKAGE ⅓-LESS-FAT CREAM
    CHEESE, ROOM TEMPERATURE

1   CUP SUGAR

3   TABLESPOONS ALL-PURPOSE FLOUR

2   TEASPOONS VANILLA EXTRACT

4   LARGE EGGS

OPTIONAL: 2 SEEDLESS ORANGES
    (UNPEELED), CUT INTO PAPER-THIN
    SLICES, FOR GARNISH

Position rack in the center of oven and preheat to 300°F. Spray bottom and sides of 9-inch-diameter springform pan with nonstick cooking spray.

In a small bowl combine cookie crumbs, melted butter, and 1 teaspoon of the orange zest. Using a large square of wax paper, press evenly into bottom and 1 inch up sides of prepared pan. Bake crust 12 minutes. Transfer to rack and cool while preparing filling. Maintain oven temperature.

Bring orange juice and ginger to boil in heavy medium saucepan until reduced to 3 tablespoons, about 12 minutes. Strain though a mesh sieve into a small bowl and discard ginger.

In a large bowl beat the cream cheeses with an electric mixer at high speed until smooth. Add the sugar, flour, vanilla, orange juice mixture, and remaining 3 teaspoons orange zest, beating well. Add eggs, one at a time, beating well after each addition. Pour filling mixture into the prepared crust.

Bake 1 hour or until almost set (cheesecake is done when the center barely moves when pan is touched). Transfer cheesecake to a cooling rack and run a knife around outside edge. Cool to room temperature, then chill at least 8 hours. Release pan sides. If desired, garnish top with overlapping orange slices. Cut into wedges. **Makes 16 servings.**

NUTRITION PER SERVING (1 WEDGE):
CALORIES 214; FAT 8.1G (SAT 4.1G, MONO 2.6G, POLY 0.4G);
PROTEIN 10.4G; CHOLESTEROL 72.3MG; CARBOHYDRATE 24.6G.

Spiced Pumpkin Cheesecake

Cheesecakes have been around for centuries, and their popularity in the United States just seems to keep growing. Pumpkin, a New World food for which tradition reserves an honored place at any Thanksgiving table, teams up with an array of spices and a crisp gingersnap crust in this creamy dessert that's right in step with the times.

1½ CUPS GROUND GINGERSNAPS	2 TEASPOONS GROUND CINNAMON
3 TABLESPOONS UNSALTED BUTTER, MELTED	1 TEASPOON GROUND GINGER
3 8-OUNCE PACKAGES FAT-FREE CREAM CHEESE, ROOM TEMPERATURE	1 TEASPOON GROUND CARDAMOM
	½ TEASPOON GROUND NUTMEG
1 8-OUNCE PACKAGES ⅓-LESS-FAT CREAM CHEESE, ROOM TEMPERATURE	¼ TEASPOON SALT
	2 TEASPOONS VANILLA EXTRACT
1 CUP PACKED LIGHT BROWN SUGAR	1 15-OUNCE CAN SOLID PACK PUMPKIN
3 TABLESPOONS ALL-PURPOSE FLOUR	4 LARGE EGGS

Position rack in the center of oven and preheat to 325°F. Spray bottom and sides of 10-inch-diameter springform pan with nonstick cooking spray.

In a small bowl combine gingersnap crumbs and melted butter. Using a large square of wax paper, press crumbs onto bottom (not sides) of springform pan. Bake 12 minutes. Transfer to rack and cool while preparing filling. Maintain oven temperature.

In a large bowl beat the cream cheeses with an electric mixer at high speed until smooth. Add the brown sugar, flour, cinnamon, ginger, cardamom, nutmeg, salt, and vanilla, beating well. Add pumpkin, beating well. Add eggs, one at a time, beating well after each addition. Pour filling mixture into prepared crust.

Bake 1½ hours or until almost set (cheesecake is done when the center barely moves when pan is touched). Transfer cheesecake to a cooling rack and run a knife around outside edge. Cool to room temperature, then chill at least 8 hours. Release pan sides.

Cut into wedges. **Makes 16 servings.**

NUTRITION PER SERVING (1 WEDGE):
CALORIES 213; FAT 8.1G (SAT 4.2G, MONO 2.6G, POLY 0.4G),
PROTEIN 10.6G; CHOLESTEROL 72.3MG; CARBOHYDRATE 24.4G.

Cranberry-Jeweled Cheesecake

WITH CHOCOLATE COOKIE CRUST

This cheesecake, a delicious contrast of sweet vanilla-orange filling, tart cranberry crown, and crisp-sweet chocolate crust, is a scrumptious conclusion to any special dinner, but especially one at holiday time.

1½ CUPS REDUCED-FAT CHOCOLATE WAFER CRUMBS (ABOUT 50 COOKIES)

3 TABLESPOONS UNSALTED BUTTER, MELTED

1½ CUPS PLUS 2 TABLESPOONS SUGAR, DIVIDED USE

3 8-OUNCE PACKAGES FAT-FREE CREAM CHEESE, ROOM TEMPERATURE

1 8-OUNCE PACKAGE ⅓-LESS-FAT CREAM CHEESE, ROOM TEMPERATURE

3 TABLESPOONS ALL PURPOSE FLOUR

1½ TABLESPOONS FINELY GRATED ORANGE ZEST

2 TEASPOONS VANILLA EXTRACT

3 LARGE EGGS

2 LARGE EGG WHITES

3 TABLESPOONS WATER

1 TEASPOON CORNSTARCH DISSOLVED IN 1 TABLESPOON WATER

2 CUPS FRESH CRANBERRIES

Position rack in the center of oven and preheat to 350°F. Wrap double layer of heavy-duty foil around outside of 10-inch-diameter springform pan. Spray bottom and sides of pan with nonstick cooking spray.

Combine cookie crumbs, melted butter, and 2 tablespoons of the sugar in a small bowl. Using a large square of wax paper, press evenly into bottom and 1 inch up sides of prepared pan. Bake crust 8 minutes. Transfer to rack and cool while preparing filling. Maintain oven temperature.

In a large bowl beat the cream cheeses, flour, and 1 cup of the remaining sugar with an electric mixer at high speed until smooth. Add the orange zest and vanilla, beating well. Add eggs and egg whites, one at a time, beating well after each addition. Pour filling mixture into prepared crust.

Place springform pan in large roasting pan. Fill roasting pan with enough hot water to come halfway up sides of springform pan.

Bake 55–60 minutes or until almost set (cheesecake is done when the center barely moves when pan is touched.) Remove cake from water bath, transfer to a cooling rack, and run a knife around outside edge. Cool to room temperature.

While cheesecake cools, stir water and remaining ½ cup sugar in medium saucepan over medium-low heat until sugar dissolves. Increase heat to medium, add cornstarch mixture and bring to simmer. Add cranberries and cook until they begin to pop, stirring often, about 3 minutes. Transfer to a small bowl and cool completely. Chill cranberry mixture and cake at least 8 hours.

Release pan sides. Top cheesecake with cranberry mixture. Chill until set, about 1 hour. Cut into wedges. **Makes 16 servings.**

NUTRITION PER SERVING (1 WEDGE):
CALORIES 286; FAT 8.9G (SAT 4.5G, MONO 3.0G, POLY 0.6G);
PROTEIN 10.7G; CHOLESTEROL 59.5MG; CARBOHYDRATE 41.1G.

Sweet Potato Cheesecake

Tangy cream cheese and yogurt are mellowed and enriched with a purée of sweet potatoes. A very grown-up splash of bourbon takes the cheesecake to an entirely new level. Using canned yams makes it especially easy to prepare.

2 CUPS REDUCED-FAT GRAHAM CRACKER CRUMBS (ABOUT 12 COOKIE SHEETS)	½ CUP PLAIN FAT-FREE YOGURT
3 TABLESPOONS SUGAR	⅓ CUP ALL-PURPOSE FLOUR
2 TABLESPOONS (¼ STICK) UNSALTED BUTTER, MELTED	1¼ CUPS PACKED LIGHT BROWN SUGAR
1 TABLESPOON WATER	1 TABLESPOON VANILLA EXTRACT
2 15-OUNCE CANS SWEET POTATOES, DRAINED	2 TABLESPOONS BOURBON OR WHISKEY
2 8-OUNCE PACKAGES ⅓-LESS-FAT CREAM CHEESE, ROOM TEMPERATURE	1 TEASPOON GROUND CINNAMON
	½ TEASPOON GROUND GINGER
	¼ TEASPOON SALT
2 8-OUNCE PACKAGES FAT-FREE CREAM CHEESE, ROOM TEMPERATURE	¼ TEASPOON GROUND NUTMEG
	3 LARGE EGGS

Position rack in the center of oven and preheat to 325°F. Spray bottom and sides of a 10-inch-diameter springform pan with nonstick cooking spray.

In a small bowl combine graham cracker crumbs, sugar, melted butter, and water. Using a large square of wax paper, press evenly into bottom and 1 inch up sides of prepared pan. Bake crust 12 minutes. Transfer to rack and cool while preparing filling. Maintain oven temperature to 325°F.

Place the sweet potatoes in the large bowl of a food processor and process until smooth. Set aside.

In a large bowl beat the cream cheeses and yogurt with an electric mixer at high speed until smooth. Add the flour, brown sugar, vanilla, bourbon, cinnamon, ginger, salt, and nutmeg, beating well. Add eggs, one at a time, beating well after each addition. Add sweet potato purée, beating until just blended. Pour filling mixture into prepared crust.

Bake 1 hour and 15 minutes or until almost set (cheesecake is done when the center barely moves when pan is touched). Turn oven off. Cool cheesecake in closed oven

1 hour. Transfer cheesecake to a cooling rack and run a knife around outside edge. Cool to room temperature, then chill at least 8 hours. Release pan sides. Cut into wedges. **Makes 16 servings.**

NUTRITION PER SERVING (1 WEDGE):
CALORIES 287; FAT 9.4G (SAT 5.3G, MONO 2.9G, POLY 0.4G);
PROTEIN 10.1G; CHOLESTEROL 66.1MG; CARBOHYDRATE 39.3G.

German Chocolate Cheesecake

"German Chocolate" does not hail from Germany. Rather, it is a dark baking chocolate created by Samuel German (hence the eponym) who thought pre-sweetened chocolate baking bars would be a great convenience to home bakers. But say "German Chocolate" to most people and they are more likely to think of chocolate cake than chocolate bars. Specifically, a layer cake, popularized in the 1950s, consisting of sweet chocolate cake layers with a cooked coconut-pecan filling and frosting. Yum. Here's my reinterpretation of said cake in extravagant cheesecake form.

1½ CUPS REDUCED-FAT CHOCOLATE WAFER CRUMBS (ABOUT 50 COOKIES)	2 8-OUNCE PACKAGES FAT-FREE CREAM CHEESE, ROOM TEMPERATURE
3 TABLESPOONS UNSALTED BUTTER, MELTED	3 TABLESPOONS ALL-PURPOSE FLOUR
1 CUP PLUS 2 TABLESPOONS SUGAR, DIVIDED USE	2 TEASPOONS VANILLA EXTRACT
	½ TEASPOON COCONUT EXTRACT
⅔ CUP UNSWEETENED COCOA POWDER (NOT DUTCH PROCESS)	2 LARGE EGGS
	2 LARGE EGG WHITES
½ CUP FAT-FREE SWEETENED CONDENSED MILK (FLOUR A 14-OUNCE CAN)	⅔ CUP FAT-FREE CARAMEL ICE CREAM TOPPING
	⅓ CUP CHOPPED PECANS, LIGHTLY TOASTED
2 8-OUNCE PACKAGES ⅓-LESS-FAT CREAM CHEESE, ROOM TEMPERATURE	⅓ CUP FLAKED SWEETENED COCONUT, TOASTED

Position rack in the center of oven and preheat to 325°F. Spray bottom and sides of a 9-inch-diameter springform pan with nonstick cooking spray.

In a small bowl combine cookie crumbs, melted butter, and 2 tablespoons of the sugar. Using a large square of wax paper, press evenly into bottom and 1½ inches up sides of prepared pan. Bake crust 8 minutes. Transfer to rack and cool while preparing filling. Maintain oven temperature.

In a small bowl whisk the cocoa powder and sweetened condensed milk until blended. In a large bowl beat the cream cheeses with an electric mixer at high speed until smooth. Add the flour, vanilla, coconut extract and remaining 1 cup sugar, beating well. Add the eggs and egg whites, one at a time, beating well after each addition. Add cocoa mixture, beating well. Pour filling mixture into prepared crust.

Bake 1 hour and 5 minutes or until almost set (cheesecake is done when the center barely moves when pan is touched). Transfer cheesecake to a cooling rack and run a knife around outside edge. Cool completely on rack.

In a small bowl combine the caramel topping, chopped pecans, and toasted coconut, then spread over cooled cheesecake. Chill at least 8 hours. Release pan sides. Cut into wedges. **Makes 16 servings.**

NUTRITION PER SERVING (1 WEDGE):
CALORIES 299; FAT 12.4G (SAT 6.2G, MONO 4.2G, POLY 1.4G);
PROTEIN 9.6G; CHOLESTEROL 47.6MG; CARBOHYDRATE 37G.

6. FROSTINGS AND OTHER

Extras

CREAM CHEESE **FROSTING**, WHITE CHOCOLATE **FROSTING**, LEMON CREAM CHEESE **ICING**, LEMONADE **FROSTING**, LIME **FROSTING**, ORANGE BUTTERCREAM, PEANUT BUTTER **FROSTING**, CREAMY COCONUT **FROSTING**, COCOA **ICING**, CHOCOLATE CREAM CHEESE **FROSTING**, CHOCOLATE SOUR CREAM **FROSTING**, CHOCOLATE LAVENDER **ICING**, CHOCOLATE SILK **FROSTING**, MOCHA BUTTERCREAM, ANGEL FLUFF **FROSTING**, DULCE DE LECHE **FROSTING**, CARAMEL **FROSTING**, BROWN SUGAR FUDGE **FROSTING**, BUTTERSCOTCH ICING, HONEY BUTTERCREAM **FROSTING**, FLUFFY BUTTERCREAM, ITALIAN MERINGUE **FROSTING**, CREAM CAKE **FROSTING**, GREEN TEA BUTTERCREAM, VANILLA CRÈME ANGLAISE, BITTERSWEET CHOCOLATE GANACHE, LEMON CURD . . .

Cream Cheese Frosting

This recipe goes with Spiced Layer Cake with Cream Cheese Frosting (page 83).

10 OUNCES (1¼ PACKAGES) ⅓-LESS-FAT
    CREAM CHEESE, ROOM TEMPERATURE

2 TABLESPOONS (¼ STICK) UNSALTED
    BUTTER, ROOM TEMPERATURE

2 TEASPOONS VANILLA EXTRACT

⅛ TEASPOON SALT

3 CUPS POWDERED SUGAR

In a medium bowl beat the cream cheese, butter, vanilla, and salt with an electric mixer at medium speed until just blended and smooth. Gradually add powdered sugar, beating until smooth. Cover and chill 2 hours before using. **Makes 2 cups** (enough to frost 2 dozen cupcakes or a 2-layer cake).

NUTRITION PER SERVING (1 TABLESPOON):
CALORIES 65; FAT 2.6G (SAT 1.6G, MONO 0.9G, POLY 0.1G);
PROTEIN 0.9G; CHOLESTEROL 8.3MG; CARBOHYDRATE 9.6G.

White Chocolate Frosting

This recipe goes with Red Velvet Cupcakes (page 99), and the cardamom variation below goes with Chai Cupcakes (page 105).

4 OUNCES (½ OF AN 8-OUNCE PACKAGE) ⅓-LESS-FAT CREAM CHEESE, ROOM TEMPERATURE	3 1-OUNCE SQUARES WHITE CHOCOLATE, MELTED
3 TABLESPOONS FAT-FREE MILK	3 CUPS POWDERED SUGAR
	1 TEASPOON VANILLA EXTRACT

In a medium bowl beat the cream cheese and milk with an electric mixer at medium speed until just blended and smooth. Beat in the melted white chocolate until blended. Gradually add powdered sugar, beating until smooth. Beat in the vanilla until blended. **Makes 1¾ cups** (enough to frost 18 cupcakes).

Variation
White Chocolate Cardamom Frosting: Prepare as directed, adding 1¼ teaspoons ground cardamom with the vanilla.

NUTRITION PER SERVING (1 TABLESPOON):
CALORIES 70; FAT 1.8G (SAT 1.2G, MONO 0.5G, POLY 0G);
PROTEIN 0.7G; CHOLESTEROL 3.4MG; CARBOHYDRATE 12.6G.

Lemon Cream Cheese Icing

This recipe goes with Carrot Cake Bundt (page 66).

¾ CUP POWDERED SUGAR

3 OUNCES (FROM AN 8-OUNCE PACKAGE) REDUCED-FAT CREAM CHEESE, ROOM TEMPERATURE

1 TABLESPOON FRESH LEMON JUICE

1 TEASPOON FINELY GRATED LEMON ZEST

1 TEASPOON VANILLA EXTRACT

¼ CUP (OR MORE) FAT-FREE MILK

Place the powdered sugar, cream cheese, lemon juice, lemon zest, and vanilla in a food processor. Process, using on/off turns, until well blended. Blend in enough milk to form thick but pourable icing. **Makes 1 cup** (enough to frost 12 cupcakes or 1 cake layer).

NUTRITION PER SERVING (1 TABLESPOON):
CALORIES 33; FAT 1.1G (SAT 0.8G, MONO 0.3G, POLY 0G);
PROTEIN 0.7G; CHOLESTEROL 3.8MG; CARBOHYDRATE 5G.

Lemonade Frosting

This recipe goes with Lemonade Cupcakes (page 89).

1 TABLESPOON UNSALTED BUTTER, ROOM TEMPERATURE

6 OUNCES (¾ OF AN 8-OUNCE PACKAGE) ⅓-LESS-FAT CREAM CHEESE, ROOM TEMPERATURE

⅛ TEASPOON SALT

2 TEASPOONS GRATED LEMON ZEST

2 TABLESPOONS FRESH LEMON JUICE

3½ CUPS POWDERED SUGAR

In a medium bowl beat the butter, cream cheese, salt, lemon zest and lemon juice with an electric mixer at medium speed until just blended and smooth. Gradually add powdered sugar. Chill 1 hour before using. **Makes 1½ cups** (enough to frost 18 cupcakes).

NUTRITION PER SERVING (1 TABLESPOON):
CALORIES 79; FAT 2G (SAT 1.3G, MONO 0.6G, POLY 0.1G);
PROTEIN 0.8G; CHOLESTEROL 6.3MG; CARBOHYDRATE 14.8G.

Lime Frosting

This recipe goes with Ginger Cupcakes with Fresh Lime Frosting (page 103).

¼ CUP (½ STICK) UNSALTED BUTTER, ROOM TEMPERATURE	2 TABLESPOONS FRESHLY SQUEEZED LIME JUICE
2 CUPS POWDERED SUGAR	2 TEASPOONS FRESHLY GRATED LIME ZEST
1 TABLESPOON 1% LOW-FAT MILK	⅛ TEASPOON SALT

In a medium bowl beat the butter with an electric mixer at high speed until fluffy. Gradually add the powdered sugar, beating at low speed just until blended. Add the milk, lime juice, lime zest, and salt, beating until fluffy. **Makes about 1¼ cups** (enough to frost 16 cupcakes).

NUTRITION PER SERVING (1 TABLESPOON):
CALORIES 61; FAT 2.5G (SAT 1.2G, MONO 1.0G, POLY 0.1G);
PROTEIN 0.1G; CHOLESTEROL 6.5MG; CARBOHYDRATE 10.1G.

Orange Buttercream

This recipe goes with Raspberry Cupcakes (page 101) and the lemon variation below with Carrot Cupcakes (page 98).

2	OUNCES (¼ OF AN 8-OUNCE PACKAGE) ⅓-LESS-FAT CREAM CHEESE, ROOM TEMPERATURE	2	TEASPOONS GRATED ORANGE ZEST
		1	TEASPOON VANILLA EXTRACT
2	TABLESPOONS (¼ STICK) UNSALTED BUTTER, ROOM TEMPERATURE	⅛	TEASPOON SALT
		1⅔	CUPS POWDERED SUGAR, SIFTED
		2	TEASPOONS FRESH ORANGE JUICE

In a medium bowl beat the cream cheese, butter, orange zest, vanilla, and salt with an electric mixer at medium speed until just blended and smooth. Gradually add powdered sugar, beating until smooth. Beat in the orange juice until just blended. **Makes 1 cup** (enough to frost 12 cupcakes or 1 cake layer).

Variation

Lemon Buttercream: Prepare as directed, substituting lemon zest for the orange zest and lemon juice for the orange juice.

NUTRITION PER SERVING (1 TABLESPOON):
CALORIES 64; FAT 2.3G (SAT 1.3G, MONO 0.8G, POLY 0G);
PROTEIN 0.4G; CHOLESTEROL 6.5MG; CARBOHYDRATE 10.6G.

Peanut Butter Frosting

This recipe goes with Elvis Cupcakes (page 92).

4   OUNCES (½ OF AN 8-OUNCE PACKAGE)
    ⅓-LESS-FAT CREAM CHEESE, ROOM TEM-
    PERATURE

⅓   CUP REDUCED-FAT CREAMY PEANUT
    BUTTER
1½ CUPS POWDERED SUGAR
1   TEASPOON VANILLA EXTRACT

In a medium bowl beat the cream cheese and peanut butter with an electric mixer at medium speed until just blended and smooth. Gradually add powdered sugar, beating until smooth. Beat in vanilla until just blended. **Makes 1 cup** (enough to frost 12 cupcakes or 1 cake layer).

NUTRITION PER SERVING (1 TABLESPOON):
CALORIES 85; FAT 3.5G (SAT 1.4G, MONO 1.4G, POLY 0.7G);
PROTEIN 2.3G; CHOLESTEROL 5MG; CARBOHYDRATE 11.7G.

Creamy Coconut Frosting

This recipe goes with Snowball Coconut Cupcakes (page 104).

6   OUNCES (¾ OF AN 8-OUNCE PACKAGE)
    ⅓-LESS-FAT CREAM CHEESE, ROOM TEM-
    PERATURE

2   CUPS POWDERED SUGAR, SIFTED
¾   TEASPOON COCONUT EXTRACT
½   TEASPOON VANILLA EXTRACT

In a medium bowl beat the cream cheese with an electric mixer at high speed until fluffy. Gradually add powdered sugar, beating until smooth. Beat in coconut extract and vanilla until just blended. **Makes 1⅓ cups** (enough to frost 12 cupcakes or 1 cake layer).

NUTRITION PER SERVING (1 TABLESPOON):
CALORIES 55; FAT 1.7G (SAT 1.1G, MONO 0.5G, POLY 0.1G);
PROTEIN 0.8G; CHOLESTEROL 5.5MG; CARBOHYDRATE 9.4G.

Cocoa Icing

This recipe goes with Favorite Fudge Cupcakes (page 90).

1⅔ CUPS SIFTED POWDERED SUGAR

¼ CUP UNSWEETENED COCOA POWDER (NOT DUTCH PROCESS)

3 TABLESPOONS 1% LOW-FAT MILK

2 TEASPOONS UNSALTED BUTTER, MELTED

PINCH OF SALT

1 TEASPOON VANILLA EXTRACT

In a medium bowl whisk the powdered sugar and cocoa powder. Whisk in the milk, butter, salt, and vanilla until smooth. **Makes about 1 cup** (enough to frost 12 cupcakes or 1 cake layer).

NUTRITION PER SERVING (1 TABLESPOON):
CALORIES 49; FAT 0.7G (SAT 0.4G, MONO 0.3G, POLY 0G);
PROTEIN 0.3G; CHOLESTEROL 1.4MG; CARBOHYDRATE 11.3G.

Chocolate Cream Cheese Frosting

This recipe goes with Chocolate Birthday Cake with Chocolate Cream Cheese Frosting (page 69).

6 OUNCES (¾ OF AN 8-OUNCE PACKAGE)
⅓-LESS-FAT CREAM CHEESE

2 TABLESPOONS (¼ STICK) UNSALTED
BUTTER, ROOM TEMPERATURE

¼ CUP FAT-FREE MILK

2 TEASPOONS VANILLA EXTRACT

3½ CUPS POWDERED SUGAR, SIFTED

¾ CUP UNSWEETENED COCOA POWDER (NOT
DUTCH PROCESS)

⅛ TEASPOON SALT

In a large bowl beat the cream cheese, butter, milk and vanilla with an electric mixer at medium speed until just blended and smooth.

Whisk the powdered sugar, cocoa powder and salt in a medium bowl, then gradually add to the cream cheese mixture until blended and smooth. Chill until ready to use. **Makes 2 cups** (enough to frost 2 dozen cupcakes or a 2-layer cake).

NUTRITION PER SERVING (1 TABLESPOON):
CALORIES 68; FAT 2.2G (SAT 1.3G, MONO 0.7G, POLY 0.1G);
PROTEIN 1.0G; CHOLESTEROL 5.8MG; CARBOHYDRATE 12.2G.

Chocolate Sour Cream Frosting

This recipe goes with Vanilla Cupcakes with Chocolate Sour Cream Frosting (page 91).

---

3   CUPS POWDERED SUGAR

⅓   CUP UNSWEETENED COCOA POWDER (NOT DUTCH PROCESS)

¾   CUP REDUCED-FAT SOUR CREAM

2   1-OUNCE SQUARES UNSWEETENED CHOCOLATE, MELTED AND COOLED

1   TEASPOON VANILLA EXTRACT

In a medium bowl whisk the powdered sugar and cocoa powder.

In a separate medium bowl beat the sour cream and melted chocolate with an electric mixer on low speed until blended. Gradually add the sugar mixture to the sour cream mixture, beating at low speed until well blended. Add vanilla and beat well for 1 minute until very smooth and creamy. **Makes 1¾ cups** (enough to frost 16–18 cupcakes or a 2-layer cake).

NUTRITION PER SERVING (1 TABLESPOON):
CALORIES 63; FAT 2G (SAT 1.2G, MONO 0.6G, POLY 0.1G);
PROTEIN 0.6G; CHOLESTEROL 2.5MG; CARBOHYDRATE 12.2G.

Chocolate Lavender Icing

This recipe goes with Chocolate-Lavender Layer Cake (page 80).

2 TABLESPOONS DRIED LAVENDER

⅓ CUP BOILING WATER

2½ CUPS POWDERED SUGAR

½ CUP UNSWEETENED COCOA POWDER (NOT DUTCH PROCESS)

6 OUNCES ⅓-LESS-FAT CREAM CHEESE (¾ OF AN 8-OUNCE PACKAGE), ROOM TEMPERATURE

Place the lavender in a small bowl; pour the boiling water over. Cover with a plate and steep 10 minutes. Strain through a fine sieve into a bowl, discarding the lavender, then cool to room temperature.

In a medium bowl whisk the powdered sugar and cocoa powder. In a large bowl beat the cream cheese with an electric mixer at medium speed until fluffy, about 2 minutes. Gradually add the cocoa mixture and 2½ to 3 tablespoons of the lavender water to cream cheese. Beat just until smooth. (Do not overbeat or the icing will be too thin). **Makes about 1⅔ cups** (enough to frost 16–18 cupcakes or a 2-layer cake).

NUTRITION PER SERVING (1 TABLESPOON):
CALORIES 58; FAT 1.6G (SAT 1.1G, MONO 0.4G, POLY 0.1G);
PROTEIN 1G; CHOLESTEROL 4.6MG; CARBOHYDRATE 10.6G.

Chocolate Silk Frosting

This recipe goes with Old-Fashioned Yellow Layer Cake with Chocolate Silk Frosting (page 74).

---

1   CUP (6 OUNCES) SEMISWEET CHOCOLATE
    CHIPS
1   12.3-OUNCE BOX NON-REFRIGERATED,
    EXTRA-FIRM LOW-FAT TOFU

2   TABLESPOONS FAT-FREE MILK
1   TABLESPOON VANILLA EXTRACT

Place the chocolate in a small, microwave-safe bowl. Heat in a microwave oven on 50 percent power for 1½ minutes. Remove the chocolate and stir until melted (return to the microwave for 10-second intervals, if necessary, to further melt chocolate).

Fill a large bowl with ice water.

Drain any liquid from the tofu, then cut into chunks. Place the tofu, milk, and vanilla in a blender and blend until smooth. Add the melted chocolate and blend until smooth. Transfer the chocolate mixture to a medium bowl and set inside the bowl of ice water. Whisk chocolate mixture occasionally until cold, about 10 minutes. Cover and chill until ready to use. **Makes 2 cups** (enough to frost 2 dozen cupcakes or a 2-layer cake).

NUTRITION PER SERVING (1 TABLESPOON):
CALORIES 29.7; FAT 1.7G (SAT 0.9G, MONO 0.5G, POLY 0.1G);
PROTEIN 0.9G; CHOLESTEROL 0MG; CARBOHYDRATE 3.5G.

Mocha Buttercream

This recipe goes with Mocha Buttercream Cake (page 84).

2 TABLESPOONS WATER	2 TEASPOONS VANILLA EXTRACT
2 TEASPOONS INSTANT ESPRESSO POWDER	⅛ TEASPOON SALT
2 TABLESPOONS UNSALTED BUTTER, ROOM TEMPERATURE	2 CUPS POWDERED SUGAR
1 8-OUNCE PACKAGE ⅓-LESS-FAT CREAM CHEESE, ROOM TEMPERATURE	3 TABLESPOONS UNSWEETENED COCOA POWDER

In a small cup combine the water and espresso powder, stirring until dissolved. Set aside.

In a medium bowl beat the butter, cream cheese, vanilla, and salt with an electric mixer at medium speed until just blended and smooth. Gradually add the powdered sugar and cocoa powder. Stir in the espresso mixture. **Makes about 2 cups** (enough to frost 24 cupcakes or a 2-layer cake).

NUTRITION PER SERVING (1 TABLESPOON):
CALORIES 50; FAT 2.3G (SAT 1.4G, MONO 0.8G, POLY 0.1G);
PROTEIN 0.9G; CHOLESTEROL 7MG; CARBOHYDRATE 6.7G.

Angel Fluff Frosting

This recipe goes with Angel Cupcakes (page 93).

½ CUP SUGAR

2 TABLESPOONS WATER

⅛ TEASPOON CREAM OF TARTAR

PINCH OF SALT

2 LARGE EGG WHITES

½ TEASPOON VANILLA EXTRACT

Place the sugar, water, cream of tarter, salt, and egg whites in the top of a double boiler set over barely simmering water. Beat with an electric mixer set at high speed until stiff peaks form and a candy thermometer registers 160°F. Beat in the vanilla. Cool slightly before using. **Makes about 2 cups** (enough to frost 24 cupcakes).

NUTRITION PER SERVING (1 TABLESPOON):
CALORIES 13; FAT 0G (SAT 0G, MONO 0G, POLY 0G);
PROTEIN 0.2G; CHOLESTEROL 0MG; CARBOHYDRATE 3.2G.

Dulce de Leche Frosting

This recipe goes with Dulce de Leche Layer Cake (page 79).

½ CUP PACKED DARK BROWN SUGAR

3 TABLESPOONS UNSALTED BUTTER

⅛ TEASPOON SALT

1 14-OUNCE CAN FAT-FREE SWEETENED CONDENSED MILK

1 TEASPOON VANILLA EXTRACT

Place the brown sugar, butter, salt, and sweetened condensed milk in a medium, heavy saucepan set over medium heat. Bring the mixture to a boil, stirring occasionally. Cook 2 more minutes or until the mixture is thick, stirring constantly. Remove from the heat and stir in vanilla. Cool before using. **Makes about 1¾ cups** (enough to frost 18 cupcakes or a 2-layer cake).

NUTRITION PER SERVING (1 TABLESPOON):
CALORIES 61; FAT 1.3G (SAT 0.7G, MONO 0.5G, POLY 0G);
PROTEIN 0.7G; CHOLESTEROL 3.8MG; CARBOHYDRATE 2.6G.

Caramel Frosting

This recipe goes with Applesauce Cake with Caramel Frosting (page 78).

1	CUP PACKED DARK BROWN SUGAR		PINCH OF SALT
6	TABLESPOONS 1% LOW-FAT MILK	2	CUPS POWDERED SUGAR
1	TABLESPOON HONEY	1	TEASPOON VANILLA EXTRACT
2	TEASPOONS UNSALTED BUTTER		

Place the brown sugar, milk, honey, butter and salt in a medium, heavy saucepan set over medium heat. Bring the mixture to a boil, stirring constantly. Reduce the heat and simmer until slightly thick (about 5 minutes), stirring occasionally.

Pour the brown sugar mixture into a large bowl. With an electric mixer set at medium-high speed beat in the powdered sugar and vanilla, beating until smooth. Cool (frosting will be thin but thickens as it cools). **Makes about 1½ cups** (enough to frost 16–18 cupcakes or a 2-layer cake).

NUTRITION PER SERVING (1 TABLESPOON):
CALORIES 63; FAT 0.4G (SAT 0.2G, MONO 0.2G, POLY 0G);
PROTEIN 0.1G; CHOLESTEROL 1.1MG; CARBOHYDRATE 15.4G.

Brown Sugar Fudge Frosting

This recipe goes with Tennessee Jam Cake with Brown Sugar Fudge Frosting (page 73).

1	CUP PACKED DARK BROWN SUGAR	⅛	TEASPOON SALT
½	CUP CANNED FAT-FREE EVAPORATED MILK	2	CUPS POWDERED SUGAR
2½	TABLESPOONS UNSALTED BUTTER	2½	TEASPOONS VANILLA EXTRACT
1	TABLESPOON HONEY		

Combine the brown sugar, evaporated milk, butter, honey and salt in a medium, heavy-bottom saucepan. Bring the mixture to a boil over medium-high heat, stirring constantly. Reduce the heat and simmer 5 minutes or until thick, stirring occasionally. Remove from heat.

Add the powdered sugar and vanilla to the saucepan and beat with an electric mixer at medium speed until smooth and slightly warm. Cool 5 minutes (the frosting will be thin but thickens as it cools). **Makes about 2 cups** (enough to frost 18 cupcakes or a 2-layer cake).

NUTRITION PER SERVING (1 TABLESPOON):
CALORIES 62.3; FAT 0.9G (SAT 0.5G, MONO 0.4G, POLY 0G);
PROTEIN 0.1G; CHOLESTEROL 2.5MG; CARBOHYDRATE 13.2G.

Butterscotch Icing

This recipe goes with Banana Cake with Butterscotch Icing (page 39).

½ CUP PACKED LIGHT BROWN SUGAR	⅛ TEASPOON SALT
¼ CUP 1% LOW-FAT MILK	¾ CUP POWDERED SUGAR
2 TABLESPOONS (¼ STICK) UNSALTED BUTTER	¾ TEASPOON VANILLA EXTRACT

Combine the brown sugar, milk, butter, and salt in a small saucepan. Bring the mixture to a boil over medium-high heat, stirring constantly. Reduce the heat and simmer until slightly thick (about 5 minutes), whisking occasionally. Remove from heat and whisk in the powdered sugar and vanilla.

Transfer the mixture to a medium bowl and beat with an electric mixer at medium speed until smooth and slightly warm. Cool 5 minutes (icing will thicken as it cools). **Makes about 1 cup** (enough to frost 12 cupcakes or 1 cake layer).

NUTRITION PER SERVING (1 TABLESPOON):
CALORIES 61; FAT 1.6G (SAT 0.8G, MONO 0.6G, POLY 0.1G);
PROTEIN 0.1G; CHOLESTEROL 4.2MG; CARBOHYDRATE 11.9G.

Honey Buttercream Frosting

This recipe goes with Bee Happy Honey Cupcakes (page 95).

---

3 TABLESPOONS HONEY

2 TABLESPOONS (¼ STICK) UNSALTED BUT-
   TER, ROOM TEMPERATURE

1 TEASPOON ORANGE FLOWER WATER OR
   VANILLA EXTRACT

⅛ TEASPOON SALT

1¾ CUPS POWDERED SUGAR

In a medium bowl beat the honey, butter, flower water (or vanilla), and salt with an electric mixer at medium speed until just blended and smooth. Gradually add powdered sugar. **Makes about 1 cup** (enough to frost 12 cupcakes or 1 cake layer).

NUTRITION PER SERVING (1 TABLESPOON):
CALORIES 68; FAT 1.5G (SAT 0.8G, MONO 0.6G, POLY 0.1G);
PROTEIN 0G; CHOLESTEROL 4MG; CARBOHYDRATE 14.2G.

Fluffy Buttercream

This recipe goes with Lemon Curd Layer Cake (page 76), and the coconut variation below pairs with Triple-Layer Coconut Cake (page 75).

1	CUP SUGAR	¼	CUP (½ STICK) UNSALTED BUTTER, ROOM TEMPERATURE
¼	CUP WATER		
5	LARGE EGG WHITES, ROOM TEMPERATURE	1	TEASPOON VANILLA EXTRACT
½	TEASPOON CREAM OF TARTAR	¼	TEASPOON ALMOND EXTRACT
⅛	TEASPOON SALT		

Whisk the sugar and water in a medium saucepan set over medium high heat. Bring to a boil; continue to boil 3 minutes, without stirring, or until a candy thermometer registers 250°F. Remove from the heat.

In a large bowl beat the egg whites, cream of tartar, and salt with an electric mixer set at high speed until foamy. Pour the hot sugar syrup in a thin stream over egg whites, beating at high speed until stiff peaks form, about 3 minutes. Reduce mixer speed to low and continue beating until the egg white mixture cools (about 12 minutes).

In a medium bowl beat the butter, vanilla, and almond extract until light and fluffy. Fold in 1 cup of the egg white mixture. Fold the butter mixture into the remaining egg white mixture, stirring until smooth. **Makes about 2¾ cups** (enough to frost a 3-layer cake).

Variation

Fluffy Coconut Buttercream: Prepare as directed, substituting 1 teaspoon coconut extract for the vanilla and almond extracts.

NUTRITION PER SERVING (1 TABLESPOON):
CALORIES 29.1; FAT 1.1G (SAT 0.6G, MONO 0.5G, POLY 0G);
PROTEIN 0.3G; CHOLESTEROL 2.9MG; CARBOHYDRATE 4.6G.

Italian Meringue Frosting

This recipe goes with Italian Meringue Layer Cake (page 72).

3 LARGE EGG WHITES, ROOM TEMPERATURE	¼ TEASPOON SALT
¼ TEASPOON CREAM OF TARTAR	1 TEASPOON VANILLA EXTRACT
1 CUP SUGAR	½ TEASPOON ALMOND EXTRACT
¼ CUP WATER	

In a large bowl beat the egg whites and cream of tartar with an electric mixer at high speed until soft peaks form.

In a small saucepan combine the sugar, water, and salt. Bring to a boil over medium heat until the sugar dissolves, stirring constantly. Cook, without stirring, for 2 minutes longer or until a candy thermometer registers 238°F.

Pour the hot sugar syrup in a thin stream over the egg whites, beating at high speed with an electric mixer until stiff peaks form. Beat in vanilla and almond extract. **Makes about 2½ cups** (enough to frost 2 dozen cupcakes or a 2- or 3-layer cake).

NUTRITION PER SERVING (1 TABLESPOON):
CALORIES 21; FAT 0G (SAT 0G, MONO 0G, POLY 0G);
PROTEIN 0.2G; CHOLESTEROL 0MG; CARBOHYDRATE 5G.

Cream Cake Frosting

This recipe goes with Italian Cream Cake (page 85).

---

1 8-OUNCE PACKAGE ⅓-LESS-FAT CREAM
   CHEESE, ROOM TEMPERATURE

1 TABLESPOON UNSALTED BUTTER, ROOM
   TEMPERATURE

1 16-OUNCE BOX POWDERED SUGAR, SIFTED

2 TEASPOONS VANILLA EXTRACT

⅛ TEASPOON SALT

In a large bowl beat the cream cheese and butter with an electric mixer on high speed until blended and smooth. Gradually add the powdered sugar, beating at low speed until well blended. Beat in vanilla and salt until blended. **Makes 2⅔ cups** (enough to frost 2 dozen cupcakes or a 2- or 3-layer cake).

NUTRITION PER SERVING (1 TABLESPOON):
CALORIES 42; FAT 1.1G (SAT 0.7G, MONO 0.4G, POLY 0G);
PROTEIN 0.5G; CHOLESTEROL 3.6MG; CARBOHYDRATE 7.7G.

Green Tea Buttercream

This recipe goes with Green Tea (Matcha) Cupcakes (page 100).

3 TABLESPOONS FAT-FREE MILK

1½ TABLESPOONS MATCHA (INSTANT GREEN TEA POWDER)

3 TABLESPOONS UNSALTED BUTTER, ROOM TEMPERATURE

4 OUNCES ⅓ LESS FAT CREAM CHEESE (½ OF AN 8-OUNCE PACKAGE), ROOM TEMPERATURE

1 TEASPOON VANILLA EXTRACT

⅛ TEASPOON SALT

4½ CUPS SIFTED POWDERED SUGAR

Place the milk in a small microwave-safe bowl. Heat on HIGH power 15–20 seconds until hot. Stir the matcha into milk until dissolved. Cool.

In a medium bowl beat the butter and cream cheese with an electric mixer at medium speed until light and fluffy. Add vanilla and salt, beating well. Gradually add the powdered sugar and the milk mixture, beating at low speed until blended. Increase speed to high, and beat until well blended and spreadable. **Makes 2 cups** (enough to frost 2 dozen cupcakes or a 2- or 3-layer cake).

NUTRITION PER SERVING (1 TABLESPOON):
CALORIES 75; FAT 1.9G (SAT 1.1G, MONO 0.7G, POLY 0.1G);
PROTEIN 0.4G; CHOLESTEROL 5.6MG; CARBOHYDRATE 14.3G.

Vanilla Crème Anglaise

This recipe goes with Dark Chocolate Soufflé Cakes with Vanilla Crème Anglaise (page 29).

3   LARGE EGG YOLKS

⅛ TEASPOON SALT

⅓ CUP SUGAR

1   CUP 1% LOW-FAT MILK

2   TEASPOONS VANILLA EXTRACT

In a medium bowl beat the egg yolks, salt, and sugar with an electric mixer at medium speed until thick and pale yellow, about 3 minutes. Set aside.

Heat the milk in a heavy saucepan over medium heat until the milk just begins to simmer (tiny bubbles appear at edge); do not boil. Remove from heat.

With an electric mixer on medium speed, gradually add the hot milk to the egg yolk mixture. Return the egg yolk mixture to the saucepan and cook over medium-low heat, stirring constantly, until slightly thick and mixture coats the back of a spoon (about 5 minutes; do not boil). Remove from the heat and stir in the vanilla. Cool to room temperature. **Makes about 1½ cups.**

NUTRITION PER SERVING (1 TABLESPOON):
CALORIES 22; FAT 0.8G (SAT 0.3G, MONO 0.3G, POLY 0.1G);
PROTEIN 0.7G; CHOLESTEROL 25.4MG; CARBOHYDRATE 3.3G.

Bittersweet Chocolate Ganache

This recipe goes with Bittersweet Chocolate Ganache Cake (page 38).

½ CUP SUGAR

⅓ CUP CANNED FAT-FREE EVAPORATED MILK

1 TABLESPOON UNSALTED BUTTER

⅛ TEASPOON SALT

2 1-OUNCE SQUARES UNSWEETENED CHOCO-
LATE, CHOPPED

1 TEASPOON VANILLA EXTRACT

Combine the sugar, evaporated milk, butter, salt, and chocolate in a medium saucepan set over medium heat. Bring the mixture to a boil. Immediately reduce the heat to low and continue to cook, whisking constantly, just until the sugar dissolves and the chocolate melts.

Remove from the heat and whisk in the vanilla. Transfer to a small bowl and cool completely. Chill 30 minutes or until thick. **Makes about ¾ cup** (enough to frost 1 cake layer or 1 dozen cupcakes).

NUTRITION PER SERVING (1 TABLESPOON):
CALORIES 70; FAT 3.5G (SAT 2G, MONO 1.2G, POLY 0.1G);
PROTEIN 0.7G; CHOLESTEROL 2.7MG; CARBOHYDRATE 9.9G.

Lemon Curd

This recipe goes with Lemon Curd Layer Cake (page 76).

½ CUP SUGAR

3 TABLESPOONS CORNSTARCH

½ CUP WATER

½ CUP PINEAPPLE JUICE

2 TEASPOONS GRATED LEMON ZEST

3 TABLESPOONS FRESH LEMON JUICE

2 LARGE EGG YOLKS

½ TEASPOON VANILLA EXTRACT

In a medium saucepan whisk the sugar and cornstarch. Whisk in the water, pineapple juice, lemon zest, lemon juice, and egg yolks. Bring the mixture to a boil over medium-high heat. Cook 2–3 minutes, whisking constantly, until thick. Remove from the heat and whisk in the vanilla.

Transfer the lemon curd to a small bowl and cover, pressing plastic wrap directly onto surface of curd. Cover and chill until cold; whisk before using. **Makes 1 cup** (enough to fill 2 cake layers).

NUTRITION PER SERVING (1 TABLESPOON):
CALORIES 36; FAT 0.7G (SAT 0.2G, MONO 0.3G, POLY 0G);
PROTEIN 0.4G; CHOLESTEROL 24.9MG; CARBOHYDRATE 7.3G.

INDEX

almonds
    Almond Pound Cake, 45
    Linzer Cake, 23
    Tart Cherry–Almond Pound Cake, 61
Angel Cupcakes with Angel Fluff Frosting, 93
Angel Fluff Frosting, 154
angel food cake, classic (and variations), 20
Angelic Raspberries and Cream Cake, 70
apples
    Caramel Apple Bundt Cake, 53
    Applesauce Cake with Caramel Frosting, 78
bananas
    Banana Cake with Butterscotch Icing, 39
    Banana-Rum Bundt Cake, 49
    Black-Bottom Banana Cheesecake, 128
    Elvis Cupcakes, 92
Bee Happy Honey Cupcakes, 95
berries
    Angelic Raspberries and Cream Cake, 70
    Blackberry Layer Cake, 77
    Blueberry Bundt Cake, 55
    Blueberry Cheesecake, 113
    Cranberry Bundt Cake, 58
    Cranberry-Jeweled Cheesecake with Chocolate Cookie Crust, 132
    Lemon Pudding Cakes with Raspberries, 30
    Linzer Cake, 23
    Mascarpone Cheesecake with Balsamic Strawberries, 118
    Raspberry Cupcakes with Orange Buttercream, 101
    Red Berries Cheesecake, 125
    Strawberry Shortcakes with Fresh Mint, 27
    Tangerine Chiffon Cake with Fresh Berries, 21
    Vanilla-Buttermilk Cake with Strawberries, 32
Black-Bottom Banana Cheesecake, 128
blueberries
    Blueberry Bundt Cake, 55
    Blueberry Cheesecake, 113
    Tangerine Chiffon Cake with Fresh Berries, 21
Bourbon-Spiked Sweet Potato Cheesecake, 134
Brown Sugar Fudge Frosting, 157
Brown Sugar Pound Cake, 45
bundt cakes, 43–66
Butterscotch Icing, 158
Cappuccino Cheesecake, 129
caramel
    Applesauce Cake with Caramel Frosting, 78
    Caramel Apple Bundt Cake, 53
    Caramel Cheesecake, 120
    Caramel Frosting, 156
    Dulce de Leche Layer Cake, 79
    Pineapple and Dried Cherry Upside-Down Cake, 24
Carrot Cake Bundt, 66
Carrot Cupcakes with Lemon Buttercream, 98
Chai Cupcakes with White Chocolate Cardamom Frosting, 105
Charlotte's Sherry Pound Cake, 65
cheesecakes, 109–37

cherries
  Pineapple and Dried Cherry Upside-Down
    Cake, 24
  Tart Cherry–Almond Pound Cake, 61
  Triple-Cherry Cheesecake, 114
chocolate. *See also* white chocolate
  about, 10
  Bittersweet Chocolate Ganache, 165
  Bittersweet Chocolate Ganache Cake, 38
  Black-and-Tan Marble Cake, 35
  Black-Bottom Banana Cheesecake, 128
  Cappuccino Cheesecake, 129
  Chocolate Angel Food Cake, 20
  Chocolate Birthday Cake with Chocolate
    Cream Cheese Frosting, 69
  Chocolate Bourbon Cake, 50
  Chocolate-Chip Angel Cupcakes, 93
  Chocolate Chip–Orange Cheesecake, 123
  Chocolate Cream Cheese Frosting, 149
  Chocolate Fudge Brownie Cake, 33
  Chocolate Lavender Icing, 151
  Chocolate Silk Frosting, 152
  Chocolate Sour Cream Frosting, 150
  Chocolate-Lavender Layer Cake, 80
  Cranberry-Jeweled Cheesecake with Choco-
    late Cookie Crust, 132
  Cocoa Icing, 148
  Dark Chocolate Soufflé Cakes with Vanilla
    Crème Anglaise, 29
  Double-Chocolate Bundt Cake, 54
  Favorite Fudge Cupcakes, 90
  German Chocolate Cheesecake, 136
  Mayan Chocolate Cupcakes, 94
  measuring, 12
  Mini Chocolate Lava Cakes, 40
  Mocha Buttercream, 153
  Mocha Buttercream Cake, 84
  Mocha Espresso Cheesecake, 122
  Old-Fashioned Yellow Layer Cake with
    Chocolate Silk Frosting, 74
  One-Bowl Chocolate Chipotle Cake, 31

  Rocky Road Cupcakes, 97
  So Very Chocolate Cheesecake, 117
  Texas Sheet Cake, 36
  Tiramisù Torte, 71
  Vanilla Cupcakes with Chocolate Sour
    Cream Frosting, 91
cinnamon
  Cinnamon Graham Bundt Cake, 47
  Cinnamon Streusel Snack Cake, 28
Citrus Angel Food Cake, 20
Citrus Pound Cake, 45
Citrus-Scented Olive Oil Cake, 52
Classic Angel Food Cake, 20
Cocoa Crème Fraîche Cupcakes, 96
Cocoa Icing, 148
coconut
  Creamy Coconut Frosting, 147
  Fluffy Coconut Buttercream, 160
  German Chocolate Cheesecake, 136
  Snowball Coconut Cupcakes, 104
  Triple-Layer Coconut Cake, 75
coffee
  Cappuccino Cheesecake, 129
  Mocha Buttercream Cake, 84
  Mocha Buttercream, 153
  Mocha Cupcakes with Espresso Meringue,
    106
  Mocha Espresso Cheesecake, 122
  Tiramisù Torte, 71
coffee cake, sour cream streusel, 59
cranberries
  Cranberry Bundt Cake, 58
  Cranberry-Jeweled Cheesecake with Choco-
    late Cookie Crust, 132
Cream Cake Frosting, 162
cream cheese
  about, 9
  Chocolate Birthday Cake with Chocolate
    Cream Cheese Frosting, 69
  Chocolate Cream Cheese Frosting, 149
  Cream Cheese Frosting, 141

Lemon Cream Cheese Icing, 143
measuring, 12
Spiced Layer Cake with Cream Cheese
    Frosting, 83
Creamy Coconut Frosting, 147
cupcakes, 87–107
Dark Chocolate Soufflé Cakes with Vanilla
    Crème Anglaise, 29
Double-Chocolate Bundt Cake, 54
Dulce de Leche Frosting, 155
Dulce de Leche Layer Cake, 79
Elvis Cupcakes, 92
espresso. *See* coffee
Favorite Fudge Cupcakes, 90
Fluffy Buttercream, 160
Fluffy Coconut Buttercream, 160
Fresh Ginger Cheesecake, 126
Fresh Lime Layer Cake, 82
Fresh Lime Pound Cake, 57
frostings and icings, 139–66
German Chocolate Cheesecake, 136
ginger
    Fresh Ginger Cheesecake, 126
    Ginger Cupcakes with Lime Frosting, 103
    Guinness Gingerbread, 37
Grand Marnier–Glazed Orange Pound Cake,
    62
Green Tea Buttercream, 163
Green Tea (Matcha) Cupcakes, 100
Guinness Gingerbread, 37
honey
    about, 7
    Bee Happy Honey Cupcakes, 95
    Honey Buttercream Frosting, 159
    measuring, 12
    Pear Pound Cake with Honey Glaze, 48
    Swedish-Spice Cake with Honey Glaze, 25
    Wildflower Honey Cheesecake, 127
Irish Cream Pound Cake, 56
Italian Cream Cake, 85
Italian Meringue Frosting, 161

Italian Meringue Layer Cake, 72
Italian Ricotta Cheesecake, 121
lavender
    about, 11
    Chocolate Lavender Icing, 151
    Chocolate-Lavender Layer Cake, 80
    Vanilla-Glazed Lavender Cupcakes, 102
layer cakes, 67–85
lemon
    Carrot Cupcakes with Lemon Buttercream,
        98
    Citrus-Scented Olive Oil Cake, 52
    Lemon Buttercream, 145
    Lemon Cream Cheese Icing, 143
    Lemon Curd, 166
    Lemon Curd Layer Cake, 76
    Lemon Lover's Cheesecake, 116
    Lemon Poppy Seed Pound Cake, 46
    Lemon Pudding Cakes with Raspberries, 30
    Lemonade Cupcakes, 89
    Lemonade Frosting, 143
    Triple-Lemon Buttermilk Pound Cake, 46
lime
    Fresh Lime Layer Cake, 82
    Fresh Lime Pound Cake, 57
    Ginger Cupcakes with Lime Frosting, 103
    Lime Angel Cupcakes, 93
    Lime Frosting, 144
Linzer Cake, 23
maple syrup
    about, 7
    Maple Sugar Chiffon Cake, 22
    Vermont Maple Syrup Cheesecake, 124
Mascarpone Cheesecake with Balsamic Straw-
    berries, 118
Mayan Chocolate Cupcakes, 94
Mini Chocolate Lava Cakes, 40
Mocha Buttercream, 153
Mocha Buttercream Cake, 84
Mocha Cupcakes with Espresso Meringue, 106
Mocha Espresso Cheesecake, 122

New York Cheesecake, 111

old-fashioned cakes, 17–41

Old-Fashioned Yellow Layer Cake with Chocolate Silk Frosting, 74

olive oil cake, citrus-scented, 52

One-Bowl Chocolate Chipotle Cake, 31

orange

    Chocolate Chip–Orange Cheesecake, 123

    Grand Marnier–Glazed Orange Pound Cake, 62

    Orange Buttercream, 145

    Raspberry Cupcakes with Orange Buttercream, 101

    Sunshine Citrus Cheesecake, 130

peanut butter

    Elvis Cupcakes, 92

    PB and J Bundt Cake, 51

    Peanut Butter Frosting, 146

pears

    Pear Pound Cake with Honey Glaze, 48

    Warm Pear and Walnut Cake, 19

Pineapple and Dried Cherry Upside-Down Cake, 24

Pistachio Rose Angel Cupcakes, 93

Plum Crumble Cake, 26

Polenta Pound Cake, 60

pumpkin

    Pumpkin Pound Cake, 64

    Spiced Pumpkin Cheesecake, 131

raisin pound cake, rum, 63

raspberries

    Angelic Raspberries and Cream Cake, 70

    Lemon Pudding Cakes with Raspberries, 30

    Linzer Cake, 23

    Raspberry Cupcakes with Orange Buttercream, 101

    Red Berries Cheesecake, 125

    Tangerine Chiffon Cake with Fresh Berries, 21

Red Velvet Cupcakes, 99

Rocky Road Cupcakes, 97

Rosewater Angel Food Cake, 20

rum

    Banana-Rum Bundt Cake, 49

    Rum Raisin Pound Cake, 63

Snowball Coconut Cupcakes, 104

So Very Chocolate Cheesecake, 117

Sour Cream Cheesecake, 112

Sour Cream Pound Cake, 45

Sour Cream Streusel Coffee Cake, 59

spice cakes

    Chai Cupcakes with White Chocolate Cardamom Frosting, 105

    Fresh Ginger Cheesecake, 126

    Ginger Cupcakes with Lime Frosting, 103

    Guinness Gingerbread, 37

    Linzer Cake, 23

    Pumpkin Pound Cake, 64

    Spiced Layer Cake with Cream Cheese Frosting, 83

    Spiced Pumpkin Cheesecake, 131

    Swedish-Spice Cake with Honey Glaze, 25

    Tennessee Jam Cake with Brown Sugar Fudge Frosting, 73

spices

    about, 10

    measuring, 12

Sticky Toffee Pudding Cake, 34

strawberries

    Mascarpone Cheesecake with Balsamic Strawberries, 118

    Red Berries Cheesecake, 125

    Strawberry Shortcakes with Fresh Mint, 27

    Vanilla-Buttermilk Cake with Strawberries, 32

Sunshine Citrus Cheesecake, 130

Swedish-Spice Cake with Honey Glaze, 25

sweet potato cheesecake, bourbon-spiked, 134

Tangerine Chiffon Cake with Fresh Berries, 21

Tart Cherry–Almond Pound Cake, 61

tea

    Green Tea Buttercream, 163

    Green Tea (Matcha) Cupcakes, 100

Tennessee Jam Cake with Brown Sugar Fudge
    Frosting, 73

Texas Sheet Cake, 36

Tiramisù Torte, 71

toffee pudding cake, sticky, 34

Triple-Cherry Cheesecake, 114

Triple-Layer Coconut Cake, 75

Triple-Lemon Buttermilk Pound Cake, 46

vanilla

    extract, about, 10

    Dark Chocolate Soufflé Cakes with Vanilla
        Crème Anglaise, 29

    Vanilla-Buttermilk Cake with Strawberries,
        32

    Vanilla Crème Anglaise, 164

    Vanilla Cupcakes with Chocolate Sour
        Cream Frosting, 91

    Vanilla-Glazed Lavender Cupcakes, 102

Vermont Maple Syrup Cheesecake, 124

walnuts

    Pear Pound Cake with Honey Glaze, 48

    Rocky Road Cupcakes, 97

    Warm Pear and Walnut Cake, 19

Warm Pear and Walnut Cake, 19

white chocolate

    Chai Cupcakes with White Chocolate
        Cardamom Frosting, 105

    White Chocolate Cardamom Frosting, 142

    White Chocolate Frosting, 142

Wildflower Honey Cheesecake, 127

✒ *Recipe notes*

_____

_____

_____

_____

_____

_____

_____

_____

_____

_____

_____

_____

_____

_____

_____

_____

_____

_____

Recipe notes

Recipe notes

 *Recipe notes*

_____

_____

_____

_____

_____

_____

_____

_____

_____

_____

_____

_____

_____

_____

_____

_____

_____

_____

Recipe notes

Recipe notes

_____   _____

_____   _____

_____   _____

_____   _____

_____   _____

_____   _____

_____   _____

_____   _____

_____   _____

_____   _____

_____   _____

_____   _____

_____   _____

_____   _____

_____   _____

_____   _____

_____   _____

_____   _____

Recipe notes

✑ Recipe notes

_____

_____

_____

_____

_____

_____

_____

_____

_____

_____

_____

_____

_____

_____

_____

_____

_____